The Hoax that Spawned the Spiritualist Cult
by
CL Gammon

Table of Contents

Introduction 1
1. The Haunting 4
2. Duesler Interrogates the Ghost 9
3. Earlier Visits by the Spirit 12
4. The "Missing" Peddler 14
5. The Spirits Take the Stage 21
6. The "Knee-ology" Controversy 33
7. The Archangel of Spiritualism 44
8. Maggie and Katie as Adults 50
9. Maggie and Katie Confess 56
10. Maggie and Katie Recant 68
11. The High Priest of Spiritualism 71
12. Ben Franklin and Other Spirits 80
13. Abe Lincoln and Other True Believers 84
14. Harry Houdini vs. Spiritualism 91
15. Others who Exposed Spiritualists 95
16. The Role of John and Margaret Fox 98
17. The Spiritualist Cult Survived 102
Conclusion 104
Selected Sources 105
About the Author 107

Deep Read Press
LAFAYETTE, TENNESSEE
deepreadpress@gmail.com

Copyright © 2025 by CL Gammon

All Rights Reserved.

The publisher prohibits reproduction, scanning, or distribution of this book in any printed or electronic form without written permission, except for brief passages quoted as part of a literary review.

Please do not take part in or encourage piracy of copyrighted materials in violation of the author's rights. Purchase only authorized editions.

The publisher does not control and does not assume any responsibility for the author's or any third-party websites or their content. Views expressed here are those of the author alone.

First Deep Read Press Edition.

Edited by: Brenda LeCrone Seaberg

Cover Design by: Kim Gammon

Cover Photo by: Kim Gammon

Paperback ISBN: 978-1-954989-69-6

Published by:
DEEP READ PRESS
Lafayette, Tennessee
www.deepreadpress.com
deepreadpress@gmail.com

For those unafraid of the truth.

Introduction

"Gladly would I embrace Spiritualism if it could prove its claims." – Harry Houdini

SPIRITUALISM is a controversial subject, and has remained so for more than 175 years. Its modern version was born on the evening of March 31, 1848. That night, the public was exposed to the Fox sisters and the rapping sounds that were supposed to come from the beyond. The interpretation of the raps was the world's first example of mediumship for sound.

The seeds sown on that early spring evening blossomed into a religious movement embraced by millions. Even though the movement went into decline about a century ago, it continues, despite the fact that the girls confessed to the hoax, and have remained discredited to this day.

Spiritualism never threatened to supplant mainstream Christianity, and it never had the eight million American followers that some claimed. But at its peak, it had more than one million adherents, and it spawned several sects based on Spiritualistic beliefs.

While the Spiritualist cult grew like wildfire, especially in the American east and throughout Europe, the faith built on the rapping sounds produced by the two girls was challenged from the beginning. The opposition continued to grow, and there were those who, like the great magician Harry Houdini, dedicated themselves to exposing those they believed were perpetrating their various frauds upon gullible people with their parlor tricks.

While this book does look at the Age of Modern Spiritualism, its focus is upon the three sisters who are responsible for it.

The genesis of the fame of the Fox girls began in a little house in a tiny town in New York, and they became a sensation in a matter of days. The prank that pulled in millions of people and generated millions of dollars made the two girls into national celebrities, like modern-day rock stars. People, some famous, wanted to see them, to touch them, to know them.

How was the regard for the Fox girls? In some quarters, their alleged contact with the spirit world was thought to be "one of the turning points of the world's history, greater far than the fall of thrones or the rout of armies."

In such an environment, it was only natural for the Fox girls to be overwhelmed by the events swirling around them. This led, predictably, to their enduring great personal problems in their later lives, including alcoholism and poverty.

This book also relates the actions of the older sister of the Fox girls and her work in promoting them, the Spiritualist cult, and herself. She was a tireless worker in the spread of the hoax, and the protection of the income she gained from it.

This volume details the confessions the girls finally gave four decades after their little prank spun out of control. Then, the reasons why the perpetrators of the prank recanted and returned to their performances are related.

This book also relates why the cult Maggie and Katie Fox breathed life into remains alive today, more than a century after those same girls discredited it.

Finally, and most importantly, this is a story of grand manipulation. The Fox girls manipulated those people who were willing to suspend their disbelief, close their minds, and embrace the tricks played on them by the pseudo mystics. Those girls grew into womanhood, changed their routine from time to time, and continued their prank for decades.

But the Fox girls themselves were manipulated. They were victimized by their older sister and others, and they felt trapped by those pushing them to continue the hoax.

There were multiple reasons for the manipulations.

The Fox girls were trapped in the prank almost as soon as they began. They, especially Maggie, continued the manipulation because they could see no way out of it.

Some believed that Spiritualism was real and true. They desired that the Fox girls spread the faith, even if the children were not completely honest in their demonstrations. Those Spiritualists felt the need to cover-up for the girls to keep them from being exposed.

There were many others who claimed to be mediums. Some of them believed they had genuine powers, others were nothing more than publicity seekers who craved headlines. Naturally, the neo-mediums seeking to imitate the Fox girls had to be master manipulators in order to surf the great Spiritualist wave stirred by the children.

There were also a large number of self-manipulators. These people simply refused to think rationally. Among this group were Americans who rose to high governmental offices. There were also best-selling authors in both the United States and England who embraced the cult. Why they chose to believe the silly shows the mediums put on are many, but the reasons don't really matter. They believed wholeheartedly.

As one would expect, the reason for most of the manipulators was greed. If money is the root of all evil, the roots of Spiritualism are deep indeed.

The Fox girls generated profits of $100 to $150 a show in 1850. In the currency of today, they would produce annual profits exceeding $1,000,000. Their older sister Leah drove them on without regard to their mental or physical well-being. Even after Leah became wealthy, she continued to squeeze out every dollar she could make from Spiritualism.

Although for most of their careers the Fox girls earned more than any other medium did, the hundreds of Spiritualists that followed close behind them made large sums of cash as well. Naturally, the lesser lights in the Spiritualist movement had to work extremely hard to top one another to keep up with their competitors.

The Fox girls, the teeming mass of Spiritualist mediums that followed them, and all the other manipulators created a false cult that still has thousands of followers today.

1. The Haunting

THERE is universal agreement that the Spiritualist cult was born in the tiny hamlet of Hydesville, in Arcadia, Wayne County, New York, on March 31, 1848. Like Bethlehem and Mecca, there was nothing special about Hydesville to recommend it as the cradle of a religious movement, but the cult was born there, nonetheless.

The Spiritualist cult began in a small, old, and nondescript wood-framed farmhouse. The small dwelling consisted of a story and a half (a single floor with a loft above). The hand hued wooden shingles on the roof kept out the rain and snow – usually. Below the floor and off to one side was a root cellar that could also serve as a storm shelter.

John David Fox rented the little house from Artemas W. Hyde, and on December 11, 1847, Fox and his family moved in. The Fox household consisted of John, his wife Margaret *Smith* Fox, and two of their seven living children: Margaretta "Maggie," age 14, and Catherine "Katie," age 10. Among their other children was a married son named David who lived about two miles away, and a married daughter named Ann Leah (referred to here as Leah) Fish, age 35. Leah was a music teacher in Rochester, New York. She would marry twice more.

The house stood among a tightly bunched group of other homes not too much different from it. Since the homes were only a few yards from one another, everyone pretty much knew everyone else's business.

According to Margaret Fox, the problem began around the middle of March 1848. On several evenings near bedtime, she heard strange noises. She said that on the night of the first disturbance, she and her husband got up, lit a candle, and made a thorough search of the house, but they found nothing. Margaret continued that she could hear the noises during the search, and that they didn't seem to move very much. The noises weren't very loud, but they shook the bedsteads and chairs, and could be felt when she and her husband returned to bed. The sounds continued until about midnight.

Margaret related that on March 30, the rapping could be heard through the house, and it kept the family awake all night. At some point, John Fox stood outside the front door, and Margaret positioned herself on the other side. Then the raps knocked on the door between them.

Margaret said that she then heard footsteps, first in the pantry, and then later it sounded as if someone was walking in the cellar. It was only then that that she "concluded that the house must be haunted by some unhappy restless spirit." The rapping and roaming about of the spirit kept her family up until about daybreak.

The next evening, Friday, March 31, Margaret said she was "almost sick" from fatigue, and she and her husband decided to put the girls to bed early and get some much-needed rest themselves. It was just past dark on that windy evening when Margaret turned in, but John was still up. Within minutes, the rapping sounds "commenced as usual," and they couldn't be mistaken for any other kind of noise.

The children, who slept in another bed in the same room, had been under the covers, but they were still awake as well. Maggie and Katie weren't afraid at all. They tried to mimic the rapping sounds by snapping their fingers. Then Katie called out, "Mr. Splitfoot, do as I do," and she clapped her hands. With that, there was a rap for every one of Katie's claps.

Sir Arthur Conan Doyle later wrote that "when the young Fox girl struck her hands together and cried 'Do as I do' ... it was, as time will more and more clearly show, one of the turning points of the world's history, greater far than the fall of thrones or the rout of armies."

What Doyle or no other Spiritualist mentioned was that "Mr. Splitfoot" is another name for the devil. The case could have been made that Katie actually summoned Satan. Naturally, the Spiritualists didn't want that conclusion to be drawn.

Margaret's story continued. She stated that when Katie stopped clapping, the rapping stopped too. Then, Maggie said with a laugh, "Now, do just as I do. Count one, two, three, four," as she clapped her hands. The spirit responded to Maggie's clapping, and it apparently frightened her.

Katie, who wasn't afraid, said, "Oh, Mother, I know what it is. Tomorrow is April Fools' Day, and it's somebody trying to fool us."

Margaret didn't believe they were being fooled – at least, not by anyone in the living world. She decided quickly that the best way to determine if the spirit was real was to question it. She asked the "noise" questions that she didn't think any human agency could answer. She first inquired about the ages of her children. The supposed spirit rapped out the ages of her seven living children, then after a pause it rapped thrice more. The three raps corresponded to the age of her youngest child, which had died.

Then the sound maker indicated that it wasn't a living human being, but rather that it was a spirit. When asked if it was an injured spirit, it responded that it was, with such force that it caused the house to "tremble."

The spirit then answered that it was injured in the house in which the Fox family lived, and that the person that injured it was still alive. The spirit told Margaret that it was the ghost of a thirty-one-year-old man who had been murdered in the house and then buried in the cellar. The spirit rapped out that when alive, it had a wife, two sons, and three daughters, but the wife had since died.

Desiring witnesses, Margaret asked the spirit if it would continue to respond if she brought over some neighbors. Margaret said, "The raps were loud in the affirmative."

John Fox didn't object to bringing in witnesses. At about 7:30, he went to the home of their nearest neighbor, Mary Redfield, and asked her to come with him and listen to the rapping sounds. Mrs. Redfield came over immediately, but she didn't expect to confront any spirits.

According to Margaret, who claimed to be calm, the children were "sitting up in bed clinging to each other, and trembling with terror." Margaret continued that Maggie and Katie were "pale with fright, and nearly speechless." She didn't explain why such a change would come over her daughters when minutes before they weren't afraid at all. Regardless, Mrs. Redfield was "amazed" when she saw the children and was convinced at once that a spirit haunted the house.

With her neighbor already certain that a spirit was present, Margaret asked it a few questions for Mrs. Redfield, and it answered. Among other things, the spirit stated Mrs. Redfield's age correctly. Mrs. Redfield then called her husband and Margaret asked the same questions in his presence. Again, the spirit answered correctly.

Mrs. Redfield then called in William Duesler and Duesler's wife. Duesler arrived at about 9 p.m. and found that about a dozen other neighbors had already arrived. Duesler then called in Artemas Hyde and his wife, as well as Mr. and Elizabeth Jewell. Besides that, several people who had been fishing in the nearby creek were also called in to witness the communication with the beyond.

Margaret took her girls and spent the night at a neighbor's house while her husband spent the night there with Mary Redfield's husband, Charles. Two of Margaret's other children also spent the night at the house. Her daughter Marie and Marie's husband Stephen B. Smith slept there. Margaret's son David and his wife also spent the night there.

Oddly, even though he was there most of the evening and then overnight, David said he didn't hear anything until April 1. Margaret commented, "How he didn't hear anything on the first evening is remarkable when so many other people did."

On April 1, the Fox house was overflowing with about 300 people yearning to hear the rapping from the spirit world. There were no unusual noises during the day, but that evening after Margaret returned with the girls, the rapping began again.

According to Margaret, the noises were heard during the day on Sunday, April 2, but not during the evening. It is interesting that, though they were considered devout Methodists, the Fox family didn't attend church that day. In fact, they seldom attended church at all.

On the evening of April 3, the rapping sounds returned. Margaret asked the supposed spirit several more questions, and it answered them to her satisfaction. The spirit put in another appearance on April 4 and Margaret communicated with it again.

John Fox supported his wife's statements. He said they searched "every nook and corner in and about the house" in search of the source of the rapping sounds, but they couldn't find anything.

The Fox family was careful to get statements from as many people as possible. Other than those mentioned above, some who confirmed they had heard the rapping were: Walter Scotten, Elizabeth Jewel, Lorren Tenney, James Bridger, Chauncey P. Losey, Benjamin F. Clark, Elizabeth Fox, Vernelia Culver, William D. Storer, and Marvin P. Losey.

The fact that they took pains to get a list of witnesses is contrary to their later statements that they didn't want to publicize events of late March and early April 1848. If they had really wanted to keep the haunting a secret, the last thing they would have wanted would have been to get statements on the record.

A myth emerged that in April 1848, a Methodist visited the Fox family. The minister proposed to exorcise the spirits from the house. He said that if the family would allow him to perform his incantations, they would hear no more of the disturbance, which he, of course, attributed to the devil. John and Margaret Fox, it was said, gladly allowed him to make the attempt. The story went that the preacher walked around the room, chanting lines that his sect often applied to cast out unclean spirits.

It was said that the clergyman was astonished and disappointed that "all his mummery availed nothing, and the spirits did not obey his commands." In fact, so said those who claimed to witness the attempted exorcism, the spirits ignored him except when he uttered "Amen." When he said "Amen," there were loud rapping sounds.

The story of the attempted exorcise is almost certainly fraudulent. While the Methodists do believe in demonic possession, they do not practice formal rites of exorcism. If the events described above did take place, the preacher was acting upon his own without sanction by his sect. Considering the insulting nature of the report, it is likely that it was fabricated to ridicule Christians – especially Methodists.

Why did so many people seem to confirm that the Fox girls had contacted at least one spirit on March 31?

First, people are easy to fool, especially when they are inclined to believe something. Second, there is no question that the doubters were faced with intense peer pressure.

It must also be remembered that the stories about March 31, 1848, were written by believers, and opposing views, if there were any, were not included.

2. Duesler Interrogates the Ghost

WILLIAM Duesler's questioning of the so-called spirit throws considerable light on the later Spiritualist movement, and the hoax that caused it to hatch.

Duesler's written statement confirmed that he arrived at the Fox house at about 9 p.m. on March 31. A dozen or so other neighbors were already there.

Duesler lived within a few yards of the Fox house, but he didn't hear any spirits or learn anything about them until Mary Redfield came to his house on the evening of March 31. Duesler related that she "appeared to be very much agitated." He said he didn't want to go over to the Fox residence, but after his wife implored him to, he consented.

Duesler was surprised that some of those present when he arrived were frightened, and that several of them refused to enter the room from where the rapping sound emanated. Duesler wasn't frightened. In fact, according to him, he laughed at the very idea that the house was haunted. Duesler entered the room and sat down on the bed. Margaret asked a question and Duesler heard the rapping "distinctly." He said the rapping was so pronounced that it jarred the bedstead.

Margaret asked the spirit if it would answer Duesler's questions, and it rapped that it would. Duesler then asked several questions, many of which Margaret had already asked. He asked if it was an "injured spirit," and received an affirmative answer. The spirit then responded that it didn't intend to harm anyone.

Duesler had lived in the house previously. He asked if he or his father had harmed the spirit's human form, and the spirit answered in the negative. But the spirit confirmed with louder than usual raps that another previous resident had harmed its physical body. When it did so, the bedstead shook more than before.

Duesler asked if the spirit had been a peddler who was murdered for money, and the spirit replied with loud raps, indicating that it had been. Through other questions, Duesler ascertained that the murder took place in the east bedroom about 1844, and the perpetrator was a Mr. Bell. The spirit indicated that the murder took place on a Tuesday night at about midnight.

Bell supposedly slit the peddler's throat with a very sharp butcher knife. Then Bell took the peddler's body through the pantry, down the stairway, and into the cellar. However, Bell didn't bury the body that night. The next day, Bell dug a hole ten feet deep, tossed the victim in it, and covered the hole with dirt.

The questioner, who by now seemed to have forgotten his skepticism, asked how much the crime had netted the murderer, and he named various amounts. When he said "$500," he and everyone else in the room heard the rapping sound.

Then, after Margaret had asked first, Duesler asked the spirit to rap his age, and the ages of several others. The number of raps matched the ages of those he mentioned. It also rapped the number of children and the number of deaths in various families.

The rapping spirit then revealed that the peddler was thirty-one years old, had five children (three girls and two boys), and his wife had been dead for about two years.

The spirit revealed the peddler's initials were "C. R."

The spirit also indicated that Bell, who was still residing near the Fox house, could never be convicted for the crime.

Charles Redfield took a candle and went down into the cellar. Duesler told Redfield to go to various parts of the cellar, and as he did so, Duesler asked the spirit if the peddler was buried at that place. After several tries, rapping was heard, which stopped when Redfield moved away from that spot. Redfield said he could hear the rapping when he was over the spot where the spirit said the peddler was buried.

After finishing with his questions, Duesler retrieved the owner of the house, Artemas W. Hyde, and brought him into the Fox home. Then Duesler repeated the same questions, and the spirit provided the same answers.

Over the next several days, Duesler questioned the spirit several more times, but his questions never varied from his script.

There are several issues with Duesler's interrogation of the alleged ghost. It appears that Duesler was answering questions that Margaret Fox had prepared and then given to him. Beyond that, later reports indicated that David Fox first asked if the spirit would provide the peddler's initials. This is another indication that Duesler was only asking questions that were fed to him. This would account for the fact that Duesler didn't ask any original questions.

Still another issue with the story is that Margaret Fox had learned most of the facts about the peddler before calling in the neighbors, and Duesler's question about the spirit's earthly job as a peddler was so out of nowhere that it was almost certainly prearranged.

3. Earlier Visits by the Spirit

EVIDENTLY, the farmhouse the Fox family moved into had a history. That is, if we believe the stories told long after the fact.

Michael Weekman, a former tenant, had occupied the house for about a year and a half. He said he had occasionally heard loud knocking and other unaccounted for noises there. They started about a year before the Fox family moved in. Additionally, Weekman said his daughter had suffered from a fearful event.

According to an account given in 1850, Weekman stated that one evening in 1847, at about bedtime, he heard a rapping sound on his door. He thought the knocks were from a neighbor coming by for a visit. However, instead of inviting the visitor to come in as he usually would, Weekman went to the door and opened it. There was no one on the other side of the door, and when he peered into the darkness, Weekman didn't see anyone on the porch or anywhere else.

The farmer wasn't concerned. He closed the door and began to undress. But before he climbed into bed, the loud knocking on the door began again. This time, Weekman rushed to the door and threw it wide open, but again, there was no one there. Believing someone was pranking him, the sleepy, partially dressed man went outside and looked around, but he found no one lurking about. Weekman returned inside, but he didn't go to bed.

A few minutes later, according to Weekman, he heard the knocking once again. This time, he went to the door and held on to the latch, ready to fling the door open if there was another knock. There was indeed another knock. It was so hard that it jarred the wooden door. Against the wishes of his family, he opened the door as quickly as he could and ran all the way around the little house looking for the trickster, but again, he couldn't locate anyone.

Weekman said the knocking ceased, and he didn't think about the strange occurrence or speak of it with anyone until the Fox family began experiencing the rapping phenomenon.

According to Weekman's story, sometime after the first event, his family was disrupted again, but not by knocks upon his door. One evening about midnight, Weekman and his wife were jarred from their slumber by the screams of their eight-year-old daughter. They sprang from their bed and rushed to aid the child.

The terrified girl told her parents that something like a hand had passed across her face and head. She continued that she had felt the spirit on her bed and all over her body, but that she wasn't alarmed until it touched her face with its cold hand. The child was so shaken that for several days she wouldn't enter the room again.

One need not recount the perfectly natural explanations available for the causes of the events Weekman described. It is also interesting that he didn't mention his story until *after* the alleged spirit visited the Fox family.

The third incident happened at about the same time as the other two. Jane C. Lape was seventeen years old, and she was the Weekman family's live-in servant. One day at about 2 p.m., she was working in the kitchen when she saw a man in the adjoining bedroom. The bedroom door was open and she saw the man clearly.

Lape had been working in the kitchen for some time, and she was certain that no one had gone into the bedroom. The only door into the bedroom was through the kitchen, and she was sure hat the man didn't go past her. Had he, she would have either seen or heard him.

The sight of the mysterious intruder terrified the teenager. He looked at her directly, but he didn't speak. Lape identified the stranger as being about average size. She said he was wearing gray pants, a black frockcoat, and a black cap. He looked like no one she had ever seen before.

Lape was so frightened that she ran out of the kitchen. Hannah Weekman had been in another part of the house when Lape saw the apparition, and when the girl returned, Hannah was standing in the kitchen. The strange man was gone and Hannah had noticed no one. Hannah thought someone had been trying to scare the servant, but the identity of the intruder was never ascertained.

The alleged visits by the spirit before the Fox family moved in were important because they added to the rumors about the mysterious peddler that was supposedly murdered and buried in the cellar.

That story follows in the next chapter.

4. The "Missing" Peddler

MOST of the stories about the spirit of the missing peddler involved it communicating through rapping sounds. However, some said it did much more. Unnamed people circulated a rumor that "the spirit of the murdered man would produce a sound like the death struggle, the gurgling in the throat ... of a man whose throat was cut; then the sound of dragging a lifeless body across the room, down the stairs, the feet striking on each step; then a sound as if shoveling dirt in the cellar, the nailing of boards, and the filling up of the hastily-made grave, — all sounding as perfectly natural as if you had stood in the grave-yard, and heard the clods descend upon the last resting place of the body of a friend."

But the rumors didn't stop there. They continued: "Another sound was produced like that of pouring a quantity of clotted blood from a pail on to the floor. This sound would come suddenly, when the family, or some portion of it, sat in a room, not thinking of the manifestations; and the first thought would be that someone had poured down a whole pailful of something, that would fall like so much blood, or, as the family expressed it, 'clabbered milk.'"

For the record, no statement by any member of the Fox family repeated the rumors above.

The family knew that confirming the story of the murdered peddler buried in the cellar would prove immediately that one or more spirits had visited the Fox home. Perhaps for that reason, David Fox took it upon himself to find the victim's body.

According to David Fox, the rapping ceased a little before midnight on March 31, and shortly thereafter, most of the crowd went home. Then, at about 1:00 a.m., he and some others went into the cellar to exhume the peddler. Since the cellar had a dirt-floor, no boards would have to be taken up.

David Fox related that he had never believed in ghosts or haunted houses before, but now, so he said, he was convinced. Before commencing, Fox asked the spirit for help. He inquired, "In what part of the cellar are you buried?" After going to each corner of the cellar without getting a response, he stood in the center of the room and the rapping began. Carlos Hyde also entered the cellar and the spirit confirmed to him that the remains of the peddler were in the center of the room.

Fox and Hyde dug down about three feet, but water from an underground stream began seeping into the hole so quickly that they had to stop without finding anything.

They returned to the cellar on April 3, and began digging again. This time, they tried to bail out the water as they dug, but they couldn't make any headway, and were forced to stop again.

Fox and his cohorts were persistent. They gave it another try on April 4. This time, Fox brought a pump along, but they couldn't lower the water enough to continue, and they abandoned the enterprise until the dry season.

About a week after the digging in the cellar ended, Lucretia Pulver gave a statement. She provided additional information regarding the identity of the alleged victim, and the man who may have killed him. She had been a servant in the Fox house when the Bell family lived there in 1844, when a peddler spent the night there.

Pulver said she boarded with the Bell family for about three months during the winter, where she worked for them part-time and went to school.

She said that one afternoon at about 2 o'clock, a "foot peddler," whom Mrs. Bell said was an old acquaintance of the family, came to the Bell home offering his wares.

The girl observed that the peddler was about thirty years old, and that he was wearing a black coat and light-colored pants. He was carrying a trunk and a basket, in which he had "vials of essence."

She overheard him talking to Mrs. Bell about his family. He told her how many children he had, but Pulver said she couldn't remember the exact number.

On the same day that the peddler came by, Mrs. Bell told Pulver she wasn't needed any longer, and that she could go home. Mrs. Bell said that if they needed Pulver again, they would send for her to come back. Mrs. Bell also said she was going to the hamlet Loch Berlin in Wayne County, New York, to spend the night. Mrs. Bell hadn't mentioned her trip out of town before.

Before she left, Pulver told the peddler that she wanted to buy some things from him, but that she didn't have any money with her. The peddler told her not to worry; that he would bring his wares to her house the next morning, but she never saw him again.

Three days after sending her away, the Bells' called her back to board with them and continue her schooling. About a week later, Mrs. Bell asked Pulver to stay out of school and alter "a couple" of coats for her husband. Mrs. Bell said the coats were too large for Mr. Bell, and that they were out of fashion. However, when Pulver saw the coats, she noticed that they "were ripped to pieces."

A few days later, according to Pulver, Mrs. Bell gave her a thimble which she said she had paid 50¢ to the peddler to get. Later, Mrs. Bell showed her some other items and another thimble she had purchased from the peddler. Mrs. Bell continued that the peddler had cheated her in the transaction. She said he told her that it was pure silver, when in fact, it was really "German silver."

German silver, also called "Nickle silver," is an alloy of copper, zinc, and nickel. The only thing silver about German silver is its color. German silver is worth much less than pure silver.

The servant girl stated that a few nights later, at about midnight, she thought she heard a man walking in the pantry. The pantry was near her bedroom, with a stairway between the two. Amelia Losey and Pulver's younger brother were spending the night with her, and they had been in bed for about an hour. The girls were not asleep, but the boy was. Mr. and Mrs. Bell had gone to the hamlet of Loch Berlin, and they weren't scheduled to return home until the next day.

Both girls were frightened by the unknown sounds. They got out of bed and attempted to protect themselves by fastening the windows and locking the door.

Pulver and Losey shivered as they perceived the man to walk through the pantry, down into the cellar, and part of the way across the cellar floor. Then the sound stopped.

Pulver stated that one morning about a week later, Mrs. Bell sent her down to the cellar to secure the outside door. As Pulver walked across the center of the cellar floor, she sank down knee deep in the "uneven and very loose" dirt. Startled, the girl screamed out.

When she got back up the stairs, Mrs. Bell asked her what she had yelled about. When Pulver told her, Mrs. Bell laughed at her for being frightened. The woman explained that the loose dirt was the result of rats being "at work in the ground."

Pulver continued that a day or two later, just after dark, Mr. Bell carried a large amount of dirt into the cellar, and he was working there for some time. He told Pulver he had been down there "filling up the rat holes."

Near the end of her time in the Bell household, she said she heard "knocking sounds under the foot of her bed" frequently. She never had an explanation for the noises. She said the household dog would sit under the bedroom window and "howl all night long."

Pulver said that the Bells "appeared to be very good folks," but she quickly added that they "were rather quick-tempered."

Regardless of her opinion of the Bells, her story implied strongly that they were responsible for the peddler's death. Her account proved they had the means and opportunity to murder the man. Moreover, by saying that Mrs. Bell accused the peddler of being a cheater, Pulver provided a motive for murder.

Pulver's story of the noises she said she heard and the disturbed dirt in the cellar seemed to confirm the idea that the peddler was buried there, and that his spirit was moving about the house.

There was other supposed evidence that implicated the Bell family indirectly. Norman Ayres and John Irish lived near the house that the Fox family later moved into. They stated that during the summer of 1844, the water in their well was "very offensive and bad." The well was within thirty feet of the cellar where the peddler was thought to have been buried. Ayres and Irish didn't say so directly, but they implied that the well water was contaminated by the decaying body in the cellar.

By July 1848, no one was living in the reputed haunted house any longer. Leah and others from Rochester visited the old house, went down into the cellar, and called on the spirits to direct them to where the peddler was buried. The underwater stream that was causing the flooding had slowed to a trickle, and the peddler's spirit, according to Leah, ordered David Fox to resume his digging.

Then, David Fox, Henry Bush, Lyman Granger of Rochester, and others, including a Mr. Post, Dr. Faulkner, and Rev. A. H. Jervis, began digging.

There was a festive atmosphere at the dig site. The women prepared "chickens, puddings, pies, cakes, and sweet-meats" for the men to have for lunch.

Leah said the "earth was hard and dry, and the digging tiresome," but that it went well. She continued that around noon, the digging crew made a discovery. After digging about four or five feet down, the crew came to a wooden board. They took an auger and bored through the plank. The auger had a broken handle, and as the person using it dropped it, it fell through the hole and out of sight.

The digging continued and a few feet further down, they found "some teeth, bones, and hair supposed to be human, and fragments of a broken bowl." The hair was "of a reddish or sandy hue" and it was presumed to be from a human head, even though no skull was found. The diggers also found some charcoal where they found the other materials. Leah said the find "showed, beyond all question, that the earth had at some time, and for some purpose, been disturbed."

The digging continued until dusk, when it was suspended for the day. Then Leah and the others went to David Fox's home. She said, "[We] were well satisfied with our day's work, and the friends felt that they had done all in their power to get at the truth of the Spirit's declaration."

The digging continued throughout the next day, but no body, skeleton, or skull was ever discovered.

The story of the retrieved teeth and bones is dubious because no one outside the Fox family mentioned the finding until years later, and only then with disclaimers attached.

Besides that, there was no evidence that any of the remains were human. The find was made after noon, after the large group had eaten, and the chicken bones discarded. So, there were plenty of bones and other animal matter about that could have been "found" and "mistaken" for human remains. And it has been confirmed that chicken bones were found at the dig site. Cooking the meal could also account for the ash and charcoal found at the scene.

Another problem was that Leah said the digging ground was hard and dry. While the ground may have been drier than in April, the stream was still active and the ground would have been moist, at the very least.

It is interesting that a number of people came from Rochester to take part in the second dig. It is apparent that Leah convinced them to come. This indicates that she was the chief instigator of the dig.

Leah stated that during the dig, a large crowd gathered, and that some of them sympathized with Mr. Bell. However, Bell's friends never attempted to prevent, or even to disrupt, the digging.

Leah said she "regretted that Bell had been named." Then she continued, "but we never knew that such a man had lived, until the neighbors had brought out the fact by putting questions which were answered by the rappings." Of course, Leah wasn't telling the truth. The questions to the phony spirits about the phony murder came from Leah's mother.

Leah certainly wanted to see Mr. Bell accused of murder. Perhaps she was just looking to promote her sisters and their Spiritualist act. Or she may have had more personal motives. Regardless of why she did it, the fact is that Leah attempted to destroy an innocent man without any evidence, except what she knew were lies.

The story of the peddler's bones wouldn't die. William H. Hyde inherited the haunted house where the Fox family had lived. Reports emerged that on November 22, 1904, Hyde discovered what he claimed were human remains in the cellar when a false wall fell down. The immediate reaction was that the bones found were those of the missing peddler from more than a half century before. It was also thought that the false wall was built to conceal the murder victim's body.

A local doctor examined the bones and found they didn't come from a single creature, but they were fragments of chicken bones, and perhaps several other animals. However, none of the bones were human. Realizing that the discovery was an obvious prank, the police didn't waste their time investigating. As for the fake wall, it was added many years before due to an expansion of the house's foundation.

A small tin trunk was also allegedly found on the site of the Fox house around 1955. The box was presumed to have been the property of the murdered peddler. There had been no connection to the box with anyone at the house in 1848. Moreover, there was no mention of a "peddler's box," either when the cellar was first investigated in 1848, or when the bones behind the false wall were first reported. Nonetheless, the remains and the tin box are kept in the Lily Dale Museum as cherished artifacts of the Spiritualist cult.

Despite the best efforts of the true believers, there was never any evidence produced to indicate that a murder had taken place, that anyone had been buried in the cellar, or that there had ever been a man such as the one described in the community peddling his wares.

The case of the mythical murder proved nothing and didn't change anyone's opinion. However, the truth is that Mr. Bell was the first direct victim of the Spiritualist cult.

By all accounts, Mr. Bell and his wife were industrious people of good character. There was never any evidence that they had harmed the peddler, if there was a peddler, or anyone else. Despite this, these clearly innocent people were unfairly shunned by the community and treated as murderers, regardless of the facts.

The rapping spirit was right about one thing: Mr. Bell was never convicted of any crime. The accusation was so ridiculous that the authorities never even investigated it.

5. The Spirits Take the Stage

MAGGIE and Katie denied that they had any knowledge of what was happening or how the sounds were produced. However, as interest in the strange happenings grew, the frequency of the rapping grew as well. The rumored marvelous deeds of the Fox girls spread "far and wide." During the two days after the first display on March 31, hundreds came to witness the girls conjuring up spirits. As a result, Maggie and Katie became famous.

Just as the news that the Fox girls were in contact with the spirit world began to spread, their older sister Leah traveled the forty miles east to Hydesville from Rochester. Leah said that in early May, she learned of the happenings in Hydesville after a friend showed her an article about her sisters. She said she decided to go there immediately. Leah and two friends, Mrs. Granger and Mrs. Grover, took the night boat from Rochester to Newark and traveled aboard an Erie Canal Erie Canal packet-boat.

It is impossible to believe that it was more than a month before Leah learned of the feats performed by her kid sisters. Yes, news traveled more slowly in those days, but upstate New York was ablaze with news of the Fox girls. Besides that, a family member would have certainly sent Leah a letter telling her of the strange doings at the family homestead long before she said she learned the news accidentally.

Leah was two decades older than her sisters and she found it easy to dominate them. Apparently, she could control her parents as well. Leah was a natural born schemer who recognized an opportunity when she saw one. She realized that the "occult" power the girls displayed was a potential gold mine, provided it was handled properly. She took charge of the girls and their business affairs immediately.

Leah began her scheme by bringing true believers together in an organization she called the "Society of Spiritualists." She then encouraged everyone to come to the newly established and suddenly famous Mecca of

Spiritualism at Hydesville, and they obliged her. Thousands made the pilgrimage, seeking the chance to gawk at the girls and listen to the rapping of the disembodied spirit that the girls could call forward at will.

The swarm of people came in wagons from every direction. Some drove through the gates, but others took down the fences and drove through the grain fields and peppermint beds, not caring about the destruction they caused. Those whose property was damaged were utterly defenseless against the hordes desiring to see the spectacle that was the Fox girls.

Additionally, like a plague, scores of mediums and spirit conjurers appeared in upstate New York. However, few could match the appearance of innocence exhibited by the Fox girls.

Leah had natural marketing ability, and she flamed the feverish fire the remarkable girls had lit. The hot wind blew across the United States and on to England, France, Italy, and Germany, as well.

Leah adroitly claimed that the girls had no pecuniary interest in displaying their ability to call up spirits. However, the girls weren't making enough by relying on voluntary contributions, and soon the "spirits" demanded that they charge admission to put on shows, and demand fees to host séances. The good news was that the true believers were happy to pay to witness the spirits at work. Later, Maggie blamed their success, at least to a degree, on the true believers. She said, "Parties came in from all parts to see us. Many as soon as they heard a little rap were convinced."

The performances at Hydesville were successful, but Leah believed she could better exploit the girls elsewhere. With the dawn of summer, Leah packed up Katie and took her to Rochester. Leah had her own daughter, Elizabeth, with her, too. However, "Lizzie," as Leah called her, was never officially added to the act.

Maggie was left in Hydesville with her mother for the time being. Katie was the more skillful sister, and Leah needed her for the act. Maggie wasn't immediately necessary to put on a good show.

Leah had made enough money from the Hydesville shows to afford better quarters. Upon arriving back at Rochester, she rented a better home than the one she had previously occupied. The house was new and had never been occupied before. Leah was in such a hurry to seem affluent that she, Katie, and

Lizzie moved in before the furniture arrived. Leah made a point of telling her landlord and her new neighbors about Katie's powers.

Word got out almost immediately that strange occurrences were happening in the new house. Katie and Lizzie let it be known that they had heard rapping sounds, and that they (Katie actually) had obtained the answers.

Then while the girls were outside the house, Leah was "aroused by that terrible sound of the pouring of a pail of coagulated blood upon the floor." The sound was, according to Leah's account, repeated three times in rapid succession. Leah claimed to be horrified by the horrible sound.

Oddly, no one seemed to question how a spirit came to be in the new house. After all, since no one had lived there before, there certainly wasn't a peddler buried in the cellar.

About two weeks after she settled back in Rochester, Leah had Margaret and Maggie come to Rochester, as well. Then, sometime later, she sent Katie and Margaret to Auburn, New York, to put on shows there.

Katie was the star of the shows in Auburn, but her mother shared the stage with her. As with everywhere the Fox girls performed, Katie's shows in Auburn caused several other mediums to appear out of nowhere.

Maggie could do shows independently of Katie only after she became proficient in creating the rapping sounds. Over time, Maggie became as good as, or even better than, Katie at creating the spirit raps.

Soon, Leah became discontented with merely managing the girls. Partly due to jealousy of her sisters' fame and partly because of her ravenous greed, Leah became a medium herself. She started her own career by sharing the stage with Maggie.

On November 14, 1849, Leah and Maggie performed at the Corinthian Hall in Rochester. A huge crowd of more than 400 true believers packed the auditorium. The presence of "investigators" was often an important part of the show, and at this event, a committee of five investigated the matter. The judges found the answers the sisters provided were "not altogether right nor altogether wrong." The hundreds of Spiritualists in the crowd found the decision unacceptable, and they expressed their contempt for the judges with angry hisses and boos.

There was a second examination conducted. This time, the investigators were true believers. They conducted their tests at a lawyer's office. During this examination, Leah performed alone, and she had no trouble reproducing the rapping sounds.

The biased judges declared, "the sounds were heard, and their thorough investigation had conclusively shown them to be produced neither by machinery nor ventriloquism, though what the agent is they were unable to determine."

The second set of tests still stopped short of being conclusive. This prompted the Spiritualists to demand yet another test to prove that Leah and Maggie had real communication with the spirit world. A third test was conducted, and this time Maggie and Katie took part. No one seemed to mind that Katie was more than 200 miles away in Albany when the show at the Corinthian Hall took place.

The girls were undressed, their ankles were tied, and they were placed on glass "insulators." After the tests, the investigators declared, "when they were standing on pillows with a handkerchief tied round the bottom of their dresses, tight to the ankles, we all heard the rapping on the wall and floor distinctly."

This satisfied the true believers, but later a former collaborator, Vernelia Culver, revealed that she had aided the girls during the test (See Chapter 9)

Eliah W. Capron, who was the principal speaker at the November 14 event at Rochester, was rabidly hostile to skeptics. He said all the critics of the cult were "bigoted and superstitious." He was especially disdainful of Henry Montgomery of Auburn, New York. Capron called remarks Montgomery made in the *Auburn Daily Advertiser* "false and stupid."

Capron also stated that the Fox children were accused of "being in league with the devil." In truth, most critics were convinced that the girls were merely frauds.

The Rochester shows were wildly popular. Hundreds of people paid 25¢ a head to attend to see the performances. The shows were pulling down between $100 and $150 a night in profits (or about $6,250 in 2025 dollars). However, Leah greedily kept all the profits for herself. Maggie seethed at being mistreated, but she was intimidated and dared not say anything about it. Despite her later attempts to break away from her older sister, Maggie was terrified of Leah for as long as she lived.

In the spring of 1850, Margaret, Maggie, and Katie began public performances at the Barnum Hotel in New York City. While they were in New York City, Leah and another sister traveled to Cleveland.

Leah had been in Cleveland with her sister for about three weeks when Margaret and the girls returned to Rochester from New York City. A few days after that, Maggie and Katie agreed to a suggestion by a Mrs. Kedzie to embark on a "western tour" where they would give "mediumistic exhibitions."

The western tour was scheduled to begin at Cincinnati, but Kedzie didn't take the girls there directly. Despite the fact that Leah said she knew nothing of the western tour before the fact, Kedzie brought the kids to see her in Cleveland. Maggie was riddled with guilt and didn't want to continue on the tour.

Leah pressured Maggie to go on to Cincinnati and eventually, Maggie agreed to go there and perform.

Leah later claimed that Maggie and Katie had gone to Ohio against their mother's wishes. That is highly unlikely, but either way, Leah sent Margaret a telegraph demanding that she come immediately to Cleveland, and Margaret came. It is apparent that Margaret was brought to Cleveland to calm Maggie down and to keep her performing.

One of the more interesting performances Margaret and her three daughters took part in took place near Cleveland at Springfield, Ohio, on May 21, 1851. However, the hosts of the séance were two local mediums: Gordon and Cooley. Additionally, medium E. P. Fowler was there.

The event took place in a room rented by New York publisher Charles Partridge. Some of those attending the séance were dedicated Spiritualists, politician and judge John W. Edmonds, editor of *The Cleveland Plaindealer* Joseph W. Gray, and fifteen or 20 others.

The séance began with Gordon going into a trance. He *then* communicated with spirits through raps and auto writing. According to Gordon, the spirits asked that the lights be put out completely. Once they were in the pitch darkness, the proceeding continued.

The few doubters who were there were not convinced by the event. One stated "a series of proceedings took place, which utterly and entirely disgusted me; of course, anything done in the dark is useless, so far as convincing people goes."

The séance lasted for about ninety minutes, during which time there was a "perfect pandemonium of noises, bangs on the table as loud as could be made by hand or foot, loud slaps, bells ringing loudly, the table creaking, napping its leaves and turning quite upside down, as was announced by the exclamations of those about it,"

Throughout the event, Edmonds did his best to confirm that spirits were present. He was constantly yelling out things such as "I'm touched – now I am tapped on my shoulder! Hear that? Now they are at my feet, now my head!" He then cried out, "They are pulling my coattails – they are pulling me towards (Maggie Fox)!"

While Edmonds was screaming, Gordon was noisily scuffing and wrestling with the unseen spirits that were trying to possess him.

Next, John W. Gray yelled out, "They have lifted him up in the air!"

Someone contradicted Gray, "No, he is standing on his chair."

Another man screeched, "Don't! I don't want to! Leave me alone!" The person then began to fight with the invisible force. The person was then dragged into a nearby closet. No one thought to turn the lights on during the supposed melee.

Gray went to the large closet, followed by Edmonds, then the mediums, and finally, all the others at the séance. What happened next, according to the true believers, was utterly absurd. Coming from inside the closet were "loud hangings, a chorus of Auld Lang Syne ... accompanied by raps on the door, and scrapings on an old violoncello, which was in the closet, violent ringing of bells, which were afterwards hurled out into the room, and then rang all around a sort of accompaniment to the music in the closet..."

The séance broke up at about 11:30 p.m., but even then the noises were still going as loud as they were when they began.

The whole story is even more unbelievable than most of those related here. The idea of a room, as dark as a dungeon, with people fighting with invisible spirits is too ridiculous to hardly mention. The story was not unprecedented, however. It is reminiscent of seventeenth century Salem Village, Massachusetts, when people claimed to have fought invisible witches.

Leah declared the shows in Ohio were "a course of triumph." As one could expect, she dropped names whenever she could. She mentioned that John W.

Gray and his wife were as strong for the Spiritualist cause in Ohio as Horace Greeley was in New York.

Leah offered proof of the Ohio triumph by relating that she was awarded a gold medal in Cleveland. Maggie received a gold medal in Cincinnati, which was later stolen, and Katie was given "a beautiful, jeweled watch and chain." Leah added that admirers gave her and her sisters "diamonds and other jewelry."

The girls fulfilled several dates on their western swing before being brought back to Rochester. Then, seeking even more income, Leah booked several shows back in New York City. She said John W. Edmonds insisted that it was her "duty" to send at least some family members to the Big Apple. She continued that "after much persuasion and deliberation," she decided to send Katie and her mother to the city for shows, while she and Maggie remained in Rochester.

It may be that Edmonds encouraged Leah to send family members to New York for shows, where acquiring gold and silver coins were her primary motives.

Horace Greeley was taken in by the Fox girls, and he grew close to the family. He gave the Fox family plenty of publicity in his newspaper, the *New York Tribune*. In August 1850, the future Democratic nominee for President published a lengthy article featuring Margaret Fox and her three daughters.

The article stated the four females had departed New York City for Rochester after a stay of several weeks. The article continued that while in New York, they had applied their "mysterious influence" to communicate with spirits. Greeley continued that hundreds of people had witnessed their powers of clairvoyance.

Greeley stated with the utmost sincerity that the Fox girls had passed every "reasonable test" and had withstood "keen and critical scrutiny."

Greeley continued: "The rooms which they occupied at the hotel have been repeatedly searched and scrutinized; they have been taken without an hour's notice into houses they had never before entered. They have been all unconsciously placed on a glass surface concealed under the carpet, in order to interrupt electric vibrations; they have been disrobed by a committee of ladies appointed without notice, and insisting that neither of them should leave the room until the investigation had been made."

The article went on by stating that "We believe no one to this moment pretends that he has detected either of them in producing or causing the rappings." Greeley told his readers that none of the doubters had "invented a plausible theory to account for the production of these sounds, nor the singular intelligence which (certainly at times) has seemed to be manifested through them."

Greeley continued with, "Whatever may be the origin or the cause of the rappings, the ladies in whose presence they occur do not make them. We tested this thoroughly and to our entire satisfaction."

What Greeley neglected to say was all spectators, doubters or not, at the performances were required to pay to see the show. Neither did he mention his home at No. 35 Nineteenth Street in New York City was occupied by John and Margaret Fox. Greeley shared the home with them when they were all in the city at the same time.

In 1850, John Fenimore Cooper, the great American novelist, was present at a private séance conducted by the Fox girls. The next year, Cooper reportedly said from his deathbed, "Bless the Fox sisters for the peace which I now feel!"

Katie and Margaret returned to Rochester after their New York City dates. Then, Leah, her two sisters, and their mother left for Buffalo on December 16, 1850. While there, Leah and Maggie gave shows, and Katie worked behind the scenes. Leah said they only intended to stay in Buffalo for two weeks, but "our friends would not consent to our leaving them so soon, as the crowded séances and the continued increasing interest seemed to demand our presence still longer." In other words, the shows were raking in wagonloads of cash.

Throughout their years on the stage and hosting séances, and because of the rapping sounds they produced, the girls were known as the world's "best sound mediums." But producing rapping sounds wasn't their only method of communicating with the spirit world. They claimed to bring forward spirits "speaking in an audible voice," and moving around furniture. The girls also claimed to feel spirits touch them. Additionally, spirits were alleged to throw blocks of wood through windows, and when the blocks were opened, important directions were found inside them. Messages written on the floors of empty rooms were said to be written by the spirits, as well.

Another way Leah and her sisters received messages was through what is called "automatic writing." Automatic writing, also called "psychography," is the supposed communication through the written word by spirits through mediums. The medium is alleged to be in a trance, usually, but not always. The communicating spirits use the hands of their mediums and cause words to be written in pen and ink. Naturally, the medium is believed to have no control over what is written.

At other times, spirits are believed to write words via instruments such as special flat pieces of wood on casters called "planchettes" or Ouija Boards.

Naturally, as they grew older, it was easier for them to use other methods of making rapping sounds than by using their worn down joints.

One important early Spiritualist was Nathaniel P. Tallmadge. He had served as a U.S. Senator from New York, and as the Territorial Governor of Wisconsin. In a letter he wrote on April 12, 1853, he related his alleged communication with the spirit of John C. Calhoun.

Tallmadge stated he had sat for several private séances with Margaret, Maggie, and Katie Fox. There were no other witnesses at the séances, but Tallmadge was adamant that he had been in contact with the South Carolina Nullifier.

Tallmadge stated that the séance table moved with no one near it. He continued that he climbed on the table and sat in the center of it. The three females sat around the table trying to help hold it down. Despite the extra weight, the table rose "and was suspended in the air about six inches above the floor."

When skeptics offered reasonable and likely explanations for the levitating table, Tallmadge attacked them scornfully. Instead of answering the skeptics in a sensible way, he called them "ignorant."

Tallmadge related that during a later séance, bells and a guitar were placed on a drawer under the table, and beautiful music emanated from them without human hands touching them.

At the séance, the three members of the Fox family attempted "direct spirit-writing." However, their attempt at automatic writing was unsuccessful except for "a few vague pencil marks" made on an otherwise plain sheet of paper.

The rapping spirits invited the mystics to attempt to receive messages through automatic writing again in a few days. The same group met several days later. Just as darkness was falling, they took their seats exactly as they had during the previous séance.

Tallmadge laid a blank sheet of paper and his beautiful silver-cased pencil on the drawer. Then Tallmadge said aloud, "My friend, I wish the sentence to be in your own handwriting, so that your friends will recognize it."

The spirit answered, "You will know the writing. Have your minds on the spirit of John C. Calhoun."

Tallmadge said he "soon heard a rapid movement of the pencil on the paper, and a rustling of the paper, together with a movement of the drawer."

The former Senator continued that he was directed to look under the drawer. He looked and found his pencil near his feet, but he didn't find the paper where he left it. It had apparently been moved by, he supposed, a spirit. When he looked under the drawer again, he found the paper and noticed that the pages were "a little deranged." He then noticed that on the top sheet were the words, "I'm with you still." Tallmadge said he and others recognized the message as "a perfect facsimile" of Calhoun's handwriting.

In some quarters, the fact that Tallmadge said he had been in contact with the South Carolina stateman held considerable weight. Tallmadge had served in the Senate with his fellow Democrat John C. Calhoun, and had known him well.

Tallmadge also claimed to have the answer to a question that had nagged him. On two separate occasions, and at separate times, he asked spirits why they communicated with the living. The first answered, "It is to draw mankind together in harmony, and to convince skeptics of the immortality of the soul."

The second answer was almost identical to the first: "To unite mankind and to convince skeptical minds of the immortality of the soul."

Tallmadge didn't seem to realize that the Fox girls had already devised an answer to the question. The answer became a standard response by Spiritualists everywhere.

Famed abolitionist William Lloyd Garrison was a devout Spiritualist. On May 3, 1854, he wrote in his newspaper, the *Liberator*, about a recent séance he attended. The eldest Fox sister was the host medium at the event.

Leah had the ten participants (six men and four women) sit in a circle. Rapping sounds spelled out words "letter by letter." The spirits (Leah said several were present) instructed her to put her feet in the lap of one of the men, and she did so. They then told the participants to wait for another communication.

Several minutes passed before any new raps were heard. Then, several spirits, according to Leah, made themselves known to be present. The spirit that sent the most messages was that of the late abolitionist Jesse Hutchinson. Hutchinson's spirit, which had seemed reluctant at first, spoke, through raps, to nearly every person at the séance.

For whatever reason, the Hutchinson spirit felt the need to prove it was real. In order to prove that no one was cheating, the women at the séance had their dresses checked by others there, and the men had their pantaloons searched. Everyone their had their feet checked as well.

Leah was also checked in an attempt to prove to everyone present that she "had nothing to do with the phenomenon, by way of fraud or collusion." She sat in such a position as to convince those present that it was impossible for her to be involved in a hoax. Of course, the people at the séance were true believers and predisposed to believe that Leah was an authentic medium.

After passing the tests, Leah had the spirit rap out the following: "I am most happy, dear friends, to be able to give you such tangible evidence of my presence. The good time has truly come. The gates of the New Jerusalem are open, and the good spirits, made more pure by the change of spheres, are knocking at the door of your souls."

Later, after bells rang, the names of three spirits, including those of Hutchinson and another abolitionist Isaac T. Hooper, appeared on the paper provided for that purpose. Additionally, from under the séance table, the spirits were supposed to have grasped the hands and feet of the people sitting there.

Adin Ballou, another abolitionist, was also at the séance. He was not as detailed in his recounting of the events. Ballou said he heard noises, and witnessed direct writing. He also said he saw tables and furniture moving about, but he couldn't say Leah didn't touch the table.

In 1857, Leah saw another opportunity to both score some easy cash, and to build the reputation of herself and her sisters. The *Boston Courier* offered a $500 prize to any medium who "could demonstrate a paranormal ability" to their specially selected committee, a member of which was renowned magician John Wyman.

Leah took her act to Boston and displayed the fabled Fox sister rapping ability. Perhaps that day the spirits weren't interested in enriching Leah any further. For whatever reason, the newspaper's committee saw through the act and concluded the raps were produced by "bone and feet movements." Leah was angry, but there was nothing she couldn't do, and she went home empty-handed.

6. The "Knee-ology" Controversy

FROM almost the beginning, the Fox girls had allowed panels to test them and judge whether or not their powers were real. The judges were usually amateurs, or worse, true believers, and the tests generally left the hoax undetected. More than that, the tests added a degree of credibility to the young mediums and generally increased their fame.

As mentioned in the previous chapter, in December 1850, Leah took her family sideshow to Buffalo where she and Maggie performed at the Phelps House. The shows pulled in thousands of rabid true believers and interested gawkers. While performing in Buffalo the act faced its first major opposition from men of science. Three professors who were also medical doctors – Charles B. Coventry, Charles A. Lee, and Austin Flint – challenged the rapping. Their study of the sounds created revealed powerful evidence that the those they called the "Rochester imposters" were frauds.

On February 17, 1851, the doctors issued a report to the press. After watching Leah and Maggie, the doctors felt a statement was necessary to "prevent a further waste of time, money, and credulity (to say nothing of sentiment and philosophy) in connection with this so long successful imposition."

The doctors stated they attended several performances by Leah and Maggie. They said they came to the Phelps House for the shows to satisfy their sense of "curiosity." The doctors observed that the performers claimed to be communicating with deceased friends and other people via "physiological explanation of the phenomena." They determined that the participants weren't actually contacting the dead.

The doctors explained their methodology. They assumed that if they could prove the "manifestations" could be accounted for "physically or physiologically" they could discount the idea of the presence of spirits. They determined that they could consider the rapping sounds were made by spirits only if they couldn't find any other explanation.

The doctors took it for granted that the rapping sounds were not made by machines or apparatuses attached to tables, doors, or other things. This was because the sounds were heard in various parts of the room.

The doctors also discounted any thoughts that Leah and Maggie used some physical object on their persons to produce the rapping sounds. This was because the two had been "repeatedly and carefully examined by lady committees." The searches precluded any idea that Leah and Maggie were producing the sounds by banging objects together, or by using other items.

The three medical men also found absolute evidence that the performers weren't creating the sounds vocally. The doctors concluded that the sounds couldn't "be produced without movements of the respiratory muscles, which would at once lead to detection."

However, the doctors found other evidence that led them to believe Leah and Maggie were faking. An indication that Leah and Maggie were cheating could be found in their facial expressions. It was evident to the doctors that creating the sounds involved "an effort of the will" by the performers. It was clear that Leah and Maggie were trying to conceal their voluntary efforts, but they failed. Creating the sounds was physically difficult, and it fatigued the females visibly.

The doctors pointed out that the rapping was always in the same room, and always near where Leah and Maggie were "stationed." This was a major clue as to how the tricks were performed.

There was no direct observation of bodily movements by Leah and Maggie. So how could they create rapping sounds without any obvious bodily movements?

The doctors thought they had an answer. They first pointed out that the "voluntary muscles" were the only ones that could be controlled directly. Manipulating the muscles would not produce sounds. but sounds could be created by the muscles acting on the body parts to which they were connected. It was a fact, so said the doctors, that joint movements could be made to create rapping sounds.

A woman from Buffalo showed the doctors her ability to make exactly the same kinds of rapping sounds as the Rochester sisters made. The woman made the rapping sounds with her knee joint.

Armed with their medical knowledge, and with the testimony of the woman from Buffalo in hand, the doctors were ready to expose the trickery. The learned men provided a technical explanation as to how the knee joint could be made to make other worldly rapping sounds.

"The muscles inserted into the upper and inner side of the large bone of the leg (the tibia), near the knee-joint, are brought into action so as to move the upper surface of the bone just named laterally upon the lower surface of the thigh bone (the femur), giving rise, in fact, to a partial lateral dislocation. This is effected by an act of the will, without any obvious movement of the limb, occasioning a loud noise, and the return of the bone to its place is attended by a second sound."

The doctors reminded readers that the rapping sounds made by Leah and Maggie were mostly double. However, the doctors continued that it was possible to make a single sound as well. One could move "the bone out of place with the requisite quickness and force, and allowing it to slide slowly back, in which case it is noiseless."

But what about the movement of objects in the room? The doctors said that the movement would occur if the object was touching – or even close by – any part of the body when the sounds were produced. They added, "the force of the semi-dislocation of the bone is sufficient to occasion distinct jarring of the doors, tables, etc., if in contact."

Continuing, the doctors said the Rochester mediums could vary the intensity of the sound, depending upon the force of their muscular contractions.

After watching "repetitions" of the acts by the Rochester mediums, the doctors were certain that the shows were fake and that there were no spirits communicating with Leah and Maggie.

The doctors added that they could provide more evidence that no spirits had been contacted, but they didn't think that providing the evidence was necessary to prove their point.

Leah called the statement by the doctors a "thunderbolt," but it wasn't a surprise. She had already been alerted that the doctors' statement "was being forged to be hurled" at her and Maggie."

The alert came to her from Dr. Thomas M. Foote, the former United States Minister to Columbia, and the editor of *The Buffalo Commercial Advertiser*.

He was going to publish the doctors' statement in an upcoming issue, and he desired to save Leah and Maggie the embarrassment it would cause them.

Foote came to her apartment one evening with the news. He was friendly and gentle toward her, but she refused to allow him inside her apartment. Standing in the hallway with his hat in hand, he advised her that she and Maggie should abandon Buffalo on the train that was leaving in about two hours. He told her the fraud had been found out and exposed. He warned her that if she and her family didn't leave on their own, they might be "mobbed out of the city."

Leah didn't accept Foote's advice in the friendly vein in which he offered it. She referred to Foote as her "oily friend" and said he had an "evil heart." Utterly offended by Foote's warning, she asked him in her "best haughtiness" what right he had to come to her apartment after-hours without notice and to try to frighten her into taking flight.

Leah slammed the door "more violently than was perhaps lady-like" in the diplomat's face, placed her key in the lock, and turned it. But she didn't stop there. She was always thinking about gaining publicity and she sensed that making a scene would draw her performances some positive press coverage. Before Foote could leave, Leah rang for the bellhop to remove the ambassador forcibly. The bellhop didn't have to confront Foote because the diplomat had no intention of remaining in the building.

Leah also told the bellhop to pass along her complaint about Foote to the hotel proprietor. Referring to Foote, she said, "that man" had visited her after hours without obtaining previous permission from her. She continued that he had insulted her, and she demanded that he never be allowed to visit her again "under any circumstances."

When speaking with the bellhop, Leah pretended that she didn't know who Foote was and said that he had never visited her before. However, she was later forced to admit that Foote "had often been at our rooms, and had entertained us with stories of the tricks of legerdemain he had witnessed in South America."

Soon after Foote's visit, his newspaper printed the doctors' statement with the headline, "The Rochester Knockings! Great Exposure of the Rochester Knockings!" Before the paper reached the newsstands, Leah had already started working on damage control. Her first step was to accuse the doctors of abusing her through Thomas Foote. She said Foote had been acting on the doctors' behalf when he "insulted" her.

Leah knew she would have to continue her offensive if she was to blunt the damming statement issued by the Buffalo doctors. Her next step to salvage her career was to ridicule the doctors. She called their observations "knee-ology." She also made the charge that the doctors weren't objective. She offered to put on a display disproving their claims. However, she wanted a built-in advantage in her favor before putting on her display.

Leah issued the following press release addressed to the doctors:

"Gentlemen – We observe, by a communication in *The Commercial Advertiser*, that you have recently made an examination of a 'highly respectable lady of this city,' by which you have discovered the secret of the 'Rochester impostors.' As we do not feel willing to rest under the imputation of being impostors, we are very willing to undergo a proper and decent examination, provided we can select three male and three female friends who shall be present on the occasion.

"We can assure the public that there is no one more anxious than ourselves to discover the origin of these mysterious manifestations. If they can be explained on 'anatomical and physiological' principles, it is due to the world that the investigation be made, and that the 'humbug' be exposed. As there seems to be much interest manifested by the public on that subject, we would suggest that as early an investigation as is convenient would be acceptable to the undersigned."

Despite Leah's demand to stack the deck in her favor, the three doctors readily agreed to her challenge. Whether or not she had been bluffing when she issued the challenge, Leah had no choice but to go forward with the exhibitions. She scheduled them to take place at the Phelps House over the next two weeks.

According to Leah, her apartment was "open freely and gratuitously to meetings of the public, or of committees appointed by them, consisting of gentlemen selected from 'the pick' of Buffalo."

Leah met with the three doctors, but only stated her opinions of two of them. Leah had kind things to say about Dr. Coventry. She called him "gentlemanly at all times and places."

Leah had a much lower opinion of Dr. Lee. She called him a "wily, deceitful man." She continued, that Dr. Lee "professed, to us, to be greatly surprised at what he witnessed in our presence." Then, she said she was later "surprised at the manner and tone of the subsequent attacks upon us in which he united." She had virtually nothing to say about Dr. Flint.

The first evening, the doctors were there for the exhibition. Also present were the proprietor of the hotel, three men and three women, all of whom were true believers in the Spiritualism cult, and several others.

Leah played the victim. She said that some of the strangers who came for the demonstrations felt sorry for the abuses she and Maggie suffered at the hands of their "cruel enemies." Leah had eventually forgotten that she had invited her "cruel enemies" to view their demonstration.

Shortly, after concluding their tests on Leah and Maggie, the doctors revealed the results to the public. They reported that the "two females were seated in chairs near each other. Their heels were placed on cushions, their legs were extended, with their toes elevated and their feet elevated from each other. The purpose of the experiment was to make the knee joints tense, and to prevent the feet from creating pressure. Leah and Maggie were left in that position for thirty minutes and no rapping sounds were made."

The doctors then repositioned the females. Maggie was moved to a sitting position, with her legs stretched out on the sofa. Leah was then allowed to sit up on the other end of the sofa. The "spirits," who at other times were so friendly to the mediums, refused to rap for them even though they were called upon several times. The experiments were proof positive that Maggie alone was the producer of the rapping sounds.

The experiment continued until Leah said that the spirits weren't coming, and that it was useless to continue.

Leah tried to explain why the spirits chose to abandon her and Maggie. Again, she played the victim card. She said it was "certainly a severe and cruel ordeal for us, as we sat there under that accusation, surrounded by all these men, authorities, some of them persecutors, while the raps, usually so ready and familiar, would not come to our relief." The truth was that Leah and her sister could only create a few "faint" raps. This was because the doctors were holding the mediums' feet and knees.

Leah continued that the doctors had angered the spirits. She said the investigation wasn't conducted in a "candid and fair spirit of inquiry for the satisfaction of an honest skepticism." Leah told those that would listen to her, and there were plenty that would, that the tests were a product of "bitter and offensive bigotry of prejudice and invincible hostility, which does not really seek, but rather repels the truth, and but little deserves the favor of its exhibition to them by the Spirits."

Leah added, "Neither men nor spirits care always to cast their pearls away upon unfit and unworthy recipients. Our spirits knew well what they could and would exhibit on the following days to the public of Buffalo and the world, through better channels of higher authority."

Beyond the fact that the doctors found them to be frauds, Leah was irritated that they didn't refer to her and Maggie by name. She said that by calling her and her sister "females" proved the doctors weren't "gentlemen." Evidently, Leah was disappointed that she and Maggie wouldn't even gain any publicity for their act.

In the next experiment, the doctors allowed Leah and Maggie to prove themselves fakes. The doctors allowed the two to sit on the sofa as they normally would, with their feet resting on the floor. The rapping sounds soon began to be heard. This was certain proof that the sounds were only present when Leah and Maggie were in the sitting position to produce them.

The two experiments were conclusive. The doctors didn't need anything else to convince them that Leah and her little sister were making the sounds themselves. However, some of those present demanded that other tests be conducted.

The doctors agreed to perform one additional test. They grasped the knees of Leah and Maggie firmly in such a way that any movement "would be perceptible to the touch. The doctors did not touch the flesh. Instead, they held the females "through the dress." This test couldn't have the impact of the other ones, because the only proof there was movement of knee-joints was the statement of the person holding the knees of the females.

The knees were held for several minutes, then released and not held for several minutes. The process was repeated over a period of about an hour and a half. The results were telling. When the knees were being held, no rapping sounds were produced. Then, when the hold was released, the spirits evidently were more inclined to communicate with Leah and Maggie. Each time their knees were freed, the rapping sounds were heard immediately. When the rapping sounds began, the doctors re-grasped the knees and the noise stopped.

Dr. Lee, who Leah had branded as "wily" and "deceitful," put Maggie to another test. He relaxed his grip on her knees "somewhat" and there were three raps produced immediately. Lee nodded his bald head and said he had felt the movement of her knee joint.

The doctors considered bandaging the knees of the females to prevent them from moving. However, "friends" of the two mediums objected to binding the women's delicate features in such a way. The doctors honored the wishes of the friends of the females and didn't perform the test.

Leah seized upon the test that wasn't performed and stated that the doctors were afraid to conduct it. She held that if the test had taken place, it would have ended in her "triumph."

The doctors concluded that the tests proved conclusively that Leah and Maggie were frauds.

Contradicting the doctors, Leah declared the tests were an enormous success. She claimed that she and Maggie had proven themselves to be genuine mediums. She also stated that she and her sister had communicated with spirits in the presence of the doctors.

Leah related that the doctors failed to disprove the gifts she and Maggie possessed, despite the help they received during the exhibitions from Dr. Thomas M. Foote. Leah, however, was still angry with Foote from her previous meeting with him, and she refused to mention him by name. When Foote died in 1858, Leah took pleasure in the fact that he was no longer among the living, saying she was happy that he had "joined the spirits."

In speaking of the skepticism expressed by the doctors, Leah said they had "put all of Buffalo on the boil." However, she held that she and Maggie had overwhelming popular support. She said her apartment was "crowded with hosts of indignant friends" during the demonstrations given for the doctors.

Leah pointed out that the demonstrations were "open and free to the public, without money and without price." But she chose not to mention that many of her "indignant friends" made contributions to her, and that the demonstrations were financially profitable to her.

For the two weeks after the doctors issued their statement of February 17, 1851, the females put on demonstrations not only for the doctors but for the "best men and women of Buffalo." These men and women were all true believers, and they expressed their conviction that Leah and Maggie were genuine. Leah was hopeful that the other demonstrations would counterbalance the scathing report the doctors would certainly issue based on the tests they performed.

Determined to blunt the findings of the doctors, on March 14, Leah released a long statement to the press. It came as no surprise that she blasted the doctors and praised her friends.

Leach wrote that she felt the need to defend herself and Maggie "against the aspersions which, if suffered to pass unheeded, might bring temporary disgrace upon the cause in which we are engaged." She added that she and Maggie were "involuntary though willing instruments of a higher power."

Leah continued that she opened her apartment to doctors Lee, Flint, and Coventry, for a demonstration to disprove their statement against her. She said they incorrectly assumed that she and Maggie knew that their performances "fallacious and unsupportable."

Leah said she had challenged the doctors to conduct a "fair and impartial investigation, believing that it was not in the nature of these gentlemen to seek our conviction of fraud contrary to evidence which I knew must convince every candid mind."

She conceded that when she and Maggie's feet were placed on cushions and "resting on our heels," there were no sounds, and when their feet were on the floor sounds were heard. But she had an explanation. The reason, she wrote, was that "our friendly Spirits retired when they witnessed such harsh proceedings on the part of our persecutors." She added that "it was not in our power to detain them."

Leah then contradicted Dr. Lee. According to her, he said, he heard two sounds when he held Maggie's knees, but Leah stated, "I counted five at one time during that operation, two at another, and three at another, which made ten instead of two." Leah informed her readers that the number of raps wasn't important. She wrote that the doctors were determined to hold to their opinion and refused to admit the possibility that a spirit might be present.

She then attacked the previous evidence that another woman had produced rapping sounds with "limber joints." Leah stated that just because it was possible to do by another person didn't mean that the Fox girls had been "thumping or snapping" their knee joints since 1848.

Leah then demanded that the doctors inform the public the condition of her and Maggie's knee joints after years of "constant service in this almost ceaseless operation." She implied that if they had been making sounds with their knees for that long, the joints would be ruined. She was relying on the fact that the public was unaware that using her knee joints in that way wouldn't cause acute damage to them. Such a use would produce no more long-term damage than cracking one's knuckles would.

Leah took another swing at the doctors. She told her readers, "I will not call this quackery, but will be content to leave it to the public to pass judgment on their professional erudition."

Leah loathed Dr. Lee, and she reserved most of her venom for him. Her contempt for Lee grew stronger after he tricked Maggie into revealing that she was using her knee joints to make sounds. The angry medium contended that doctors Coventry and Flint were virtually uninvolved in the investigation, and that it was Lee that visited her apartment frequently. She stated that Dr. Lee "several times expressed great surprise, affirming, with great apparent candor, that the sounds were truly astonishing."

Calling Dr. Lee a liar, Leah stated that he had witnessed the spirits providing correct answers to questions and stated that he had no explanation for them. She challenged Dr. Lee to tell the public how the spirits answered the questions correctly.

Leah, speaking for the spirits, contended that they had previously given the answers but refused to do so later, because the original questioner was in close communication with Dr. Lee. Leah said, "Spirits associate by affinity," and they would not associate with any of Dr. Lee's friends.

Leah used the presence of Dr. Lee as the reason that the spirits wouldn't come before the doctors, and why she wouldn't call on them to do so. "I do not believe the Spirits of my dear departed friends could manifest themselves in their presence, and I would not willingly call on them to mingle in such society," she wrote.

Leah also condemned Dr. Lee, who was the editor of the *Buffalo Medical Journal*, for publishing an "injurious report against our moral integrity." She demanded that he make "reparation as apparent as the injury."

Leah took especial offense at being called an imposter. She feared the "cruel charge" would "naturally excite in every human bosom" the belief that she was a fraud. She said that she demanded "justice at the hands of a discerning public." Despite all her charges, Leah never demonstrated any proof that Dr. Lee and the others were wrong in their assessment that she and her sisters were pretending to call up spirits.

The facts notwithstanding, Leah again pointed out the "committees" that had witnessed her shows had declared them an "entire success." She again failed to mention that the committees were made up of her friends and supporters. One of those Leah mentioned was former U.S. Senator Nathaniel Pitcher Tallmadge. As was related earlier in this volume, Tallmadge was a dedicated Spiritualist, and he was anything but objective.

Leah recounted performances which hadn't been reported upon at the time. She said the exhibitions followed almost the same pattern as the tests conducted by the doctors. However, in those instances, not only did the spirits appear, but they did so in abundance. Leah claimed that she had never met most of the committee members, which may have been true. However, Leah knew all of the committee leaders, and they were disposed to believe that she and Maggie were genuine mediums.

She challenged doctors Lee, Flint, and Coventry to "club their professional lore," and explain how "bells are rung, and gongs made to ring out tunes, untouched by human hands; for, if you have any confidence in your own citizens, they can tell you what I now affirm is true."

Of course, the doctors could explain it. No bells had rung, or gongs had played any tunes while they were present. The unanswered question remained: why wouldn't bells ring or gongs play tunes when objective observers were present?

The compelling evidence the doctors obtained that proved Leah and Maggie were fakers meant nothing. As usual, science could not penetrate the humbug. The imposters remained largely unscathed, and the Spiritualist cult wasn't greatly harmed by the Buffalo doctors.

7. The Archangel of Spiritualism

INVARIABLY, modern religious cults have charismatic founders, and Spiritualism was no different. The true founder of the Spiritualist faith was the eldest Fox daughter Leah. Leah has been mentioned several times in this volume already, but her importance to the Spiritualist cult necessitates that a chapter be devoted to her.

Leah was different from other cult founders in some respects. Historically, founders of religions control a specific sect. Leah did not. The sect she tried to create and head, failed. Her personality was simply not strong enough to do what John Smith and Brigham Young were able to accomplish.

Another difference was that cult founders tend to believe their faiths are genuine, but that was not the case with Leah. She knew Spiritualism was phony from the outset, and she milked the gullible for every cent she could squeeze out of them.

Born Ann Leah Fox, she married three times. Her first husband was named Bowman Fish. Leah was much younger than Fish, and the marriage didn't last. She admitted that after her husband learned she had deceived him about her age, he became "indifferent to his home and family." Leah continued that her husband went out west on business, and he never returned. She said she learned later that he had married a wealthy woman in Illinois.

Leah's second husband was Calvin Brown. Brown had lived with the Fox family for several years, and he was considered a member of their family. Eventually, he and Leah entered into a relationship.

Leah and Brown married on September 10, 1851, while he was thought to be on his deathbed. However, Brown lingered for more than a year and a half. His condition remained stable until the end of 1852, when he grew worse. Brown died on May 4, 1853, leaving Leah a widow. However, she was busy promoting the careers of herself and her sisters, and she didn't use much time grieving.

The question remains as to exactly why Leah agreed to marry an extremely sick man, eleven years her junior, who would be dead soon. The answer isn't discernable, but considering her other antics, it wouldn't be a surprise if she had motives other than love when she wed the invalid.

Finally, Leah married a wealthy "Wall Street insurance magnate" named David Underhill on November 2, 1858. Greed isn't tempered by wealth, and even though her third marriage was to a rich man, the suddenly wealthy Leah continued to milk the golden cash cow that was Spiritualism. Underhill was more than willing for Leah to continue her career. He had been a Spiritualist true believer for years before he and Leah were wed.

A few years before David Underhill married Leah, he was involved in a major case which had its origins on Christmas Eve, 1852. That evening, Underhill attended an Episcopal Church in Massillon, Ohio, with a medium named Abby Warner. Underhill later said that the "spirits had directed Abby to go to church" with the purpose of their manifesting themselves there and taking advantage of the "favorable theater."

Soon after the service began, loud rapping sounds could be heard in the church. The clergyman leading the service asked for the noise to stop, and it did, but only for a few minutes. Then, the rapping sounds resumed, even louder than before. It was established that the sounds were coming from where Warner was seated.

She wouldn't stop the sounds, and she was arrested on a charge of disturbing a religious meeting. Warner's defense was that even though the sounds "occurred in her presence, they were not made by her conscious agency, nor were they under her control."

At Abby's trial the court ruled there was insufficient evidence to prove that Warner had intentionally disrupted the church service, and she wasn't convicted. The Spiritualists declared victory. They claimed falsely that the court ruling recognized that spirits had made the sounds.

About a year later, Underhill pushed the perceived Spiritualist victory too far. He filed a libel suit against those that charged Warner. The jury in the case was unconvinced that spirits had disrupted the church service, or that Warner had suffered any noticeable harm. The jury spent little time in deliberation before ruling against Underhill and Warner.

Overall, the case was a victory for Spiritualism in the respect that it gained publicity for the cult.

Leah was 35 years old and single when her sisters, whom she barely knew, began to amaze their neighbors with their rapping. She may or may not have been part of the original fakery, but she certainly knew how to exploit it. She had a genius for organization, and she was adept at fraud.

Leah took over the careers of the Fox sisters. She did all the scheduling and collected all the income.

The girls experienced immediate success. The public displays Leah organized at Hydesville helped create a stir across New York and elsewhere, just as Leah hoped it would.

She said, "we were greatly favored in our early associations with a class of progressive philanthropic people among our neighbors, whose highest aim was to benefit the world, and who urged us to go forth and do our duty." She also stated that after seeing her brother "bow with the others, and ask questions of the Spirits" felt her "soul ... was lifted." Since her entire promotion of Spiritualism was hogwash, she must have been buoyed by the fact that if she could deceive her brother, she could fool anyone.

Despite the fact that the previously mentioned Buffalo doctors tried their best, Leah peddled her wares to true believers for decades without slowing down. Her scheming may never have been found out had her sisters not finally exposed her four decades after she began to weave of web of deception (see Chapter 9).

Leah understood that to maintain their appeal to Spiritualists, she had to develop new techniques, or the shows would become stale. Leah knew that if the audience became bored with the product, they'd stop paying for the shows.

In 1869, Leah, with the help of her sister Katie, added another feature to her performances. She suddenly developed the ability to "raise up" a physical ghost from the eerie mists of the netherworld. In the darkness – her ghostly friends refused to appear in the good light – a glowing, veil-wearing female ghost (played by Katie) would walk around the room.

None of the true believers that witnessed the scene seemed to question why the ghost was held firmly to the floor by gravity rather than floating through the air. Nor did they wonder why the ghost gave off the unmistakable smell of phosphorus (the material that made the veil glow).

Perhaps, as one might suspect, as they gradually improved their act, the Fox family inadvertently created a series of deceptions for other Spiritualists to emulate and apply. To this day, séances still follow the same basic formula that the Fox girls introduced in 1848.

A few months after Leah introduced the walking ghost to her act, Estelle Livermore died. Estelle was the wife of a rich New York banker named Charles Livermore. He was distraught and he sought out a medium who would help him contact his wife. Livermore had attended shows put on by the Fox sisters before, and when Leah offered to help him, he happily accepted.

At the first séance with Livermore, not only did Leah convince him that she had summoned his wife, but as an added bonus, she also had Benjamin Franklin converse with the sad banker.

Over a period of six years, Leah and Katie had some 400 private séances with Livermore. In each of them, Katie Fox played the role of Livermore's wife. Apparently, the wealthy banker never caught on to the deception.

While Leah knew full-well that Spiritualism was false, she tried to convince everyone, even her sisters, that spirits were real, and that she could contact them. Beyond that, beginning sometime around 1855, and continuing for most of the remainder of her life, she endeavored to use the remnants of the Society of Spiritualists to create her own "personality cult," but, like her walking ghost, it never got off the ground.

Leah's efforts to convince her sisters that Spiritualism was real didn't have any effect on Maggie and Katie. They knew all too well that they were fakes, and that their shows had no religious significance. They also knew they were the tools of their older sister, and they resented her for the way she treated them.

Maggie explained how Leah controlled the two younger sisters. "Katie and I were led around like lambs. We went to New York from Rochester and then all over the United States. We drew immense crowds. I remember particularly Cincinnati. We stopped at the Burnett House. The rooms were jammed from morning till night and we were called upon by those old wretches to show our rappings when we should have been out at play in the fresh air."

There have been those, before and since, who have founded religious sects for altruistic reasons. However, Leah's only interest was to gain wealth and fame. Despite the fact that she failed to establish a sect of her own, Leah did succeed at pushing the Spiritualist cult generally, and it wouldn't exist today without her trickery.

Leah was vindictive and litigious. She often threatened legal action against those who opposed her, while at the same time playing victim. She seemed to always believe that a mob was just around the corner waiting to attack her and her two meal tickets. The fact was that no one ever prevented the shows she and her sisters put on, and none of them were ever in serious danger.

Leah was willing to get down and dirty with her opponents. One of them was abolitionist Charles Chauncey Burr. Burr, a good friend of Edgar Allen Poe, was extremely critical of Spiritualism, and especially of Leah and her sisters.

Burr was able to produce raps identical to those produced by Leah and her sisters. He made the sounds with one toe and the sole of one foot. The effect was similar to snapping one's fingers. Burr's brother, Herman, could also reproduce the sounds Leah and her sisters said were from the beyond.

Leah said that at first she was indifferent to Burr's attacks, but that wasn't true. She later admitted that as of 1850, Burr was her "arch enemy." Leah made sure to send someone out after every speech Burr made to challenge his statements. Leah and her Spiritualist allies ridiculed Burr's ability to make the sounds, calling them "toe-ology." They also said Burr's method of producing sounds was a "miserable trick."

Leah encouraged the Spiritualists to act against Burr with violence, and they responded. She cackled that Burr's speech at Painesville, Ohio, was met with "showers of eggs and muddy pieces of turf." She continued that the next day, Burr was "almost hooted and pelted out of the State."

Leah also tried to make the point that she and her sisters were identifying the spirits that were "rapping" to them. Of course, if they were faking the rapping sounds, they were also faking the identification of the spirits.

Leah was perfectly willing to turn on her sisters when they displeased her. After Maggie escaped her clutches in 1876 and went to England to live with Katie, Leah was enraged and she promised to get revenge.

As will be related in the next chapter, Leah threatened retribution against Maggie and went as far as causing Katie's arrest. Then, Leah tried unsuccessfully to have a court take Katie's children from her.

Leah was listed as the author of the 1885 book titled *The Missing Link in Modern Spiritualism*. Leah didn't write it, but she approved of its contents. The book is of value only to the degree that illustrates her desire to be seen as the world's greatest Spiritualist, and history's most persecuted Spiritualist.

It is interesting that the title of her book, *The Missing Link in Modern Spiritualism* tied it subliminally to the theory of evolution as first postulated by Charles Darwin in 1858.

In 1885, the evolutionists were searching for a "missing link" that would prove a common ancestor of humans and apes. Leah's book was possibly intended to hint that the Spiritualist cult had scientific validity. Then again, it may have been titled that way to take a swipe at Christianity.

8. Maggie and Katie as Adults

AFTER the girls had toured for a time, their friend Horace Greeley sent Katie to school at his expense.

Without Katie, Maggie continued her career, sometimes solo, sometimes with her sister Leah, and sometimes with her mother. With the aid of her mother, Maggie held a series of séances at the Union Hotel in Philadelphia where they had taken up residence.

Maggie was doing well professionally, but the beautiful twenty-year-old woman was lonely, drinking heavily, and was ravished with guilt. Then in 1852, Maggie's life took an upward turn when she met the swashbuckling Arctic explorer Dr. Elisha Kent Kane.

Kane was 33. He came from a wealthy Philadelphia family. His father was a judge, and his mother was an aristocrat. After illness ended his plans to become an engineer, Kane entered the University of Pennsylvania Medical School and graduated in 1842. He soon became an assistant surgeon in the United States Navy, which satisfied his wanderlust for a while. He had the opportunity to visit Bombay, Macao, Madeira, and Rio de Janeiro.

Kane then went to China under the command of Admiral Caleb Cushing, where he served as "surgeon of the embassy." He also traveled through Greece on foot, sailed up the Nile, did a tour of India, Ceylon, and the South Sea Islands, explored the Philippine island of Luzon, and even climbed the Himalayas. He also served in the Mexican-American War. His thirst for adventure still unquenched, he took part in two arctic explorations.

Kane fell in love with the highly attractive Maggie Fox, but she was below his rank, and his parents didn't approve of her. The explorer thought if he could get her educated, he could make Maggie more acceptable to his blueblood parents. He placed Maggie in a school at Philadelphia. Not only was she to take basic academic courses, but she was expected to learn French, German, and Italian, and to study vocal and instrumental music. In later years, Maggie's rudimentary knowledge of foreign languages helped her converse with "spirits" that didn't speak English.

As long as they were together, Kane forbade his wife from practicing her trade. He was a Christian and it was natural for him to reject the anti-Christian views espoused by the Spiritualists. Beyond that, he could see the fraud clearly, and he was determined to pull Maggie away from her deceit and hypocrisy.

Maggie's lover knew that she was not the instigator of the continuing fraud. It was clear to him that Leah was the mastermind behind the hoax, and that the girls were her puppets.

Kane also attempted to save Katie. He wrote to her, "Take my advice and never talk of the spirits either to friends or strangers. You know that with all my intimacy with Maggie after a whole month's trial I could make nothing of them."

It is interesting that Maggie, who had fooled thousands instantly, couldn't trick Kane even after trying to every day for a month.

Kane was also concerned about the excessive drinking Maggie and Katie were doing. He wrote to Maggie: "Tell Katie to drink no champagne, and you follow the same advice."

Maggie was out of public view for the next three years, and during that time she became a Roman Catholic. However, she continued to drink heavily.

The arctic explorations ruined Kane's already fragile health, and he left America to try to regain his vigor. Maggie said she was to join Kane overseas, but he died at Havana, Cuba, on February 16, 1857.

Maggie said that she and Kane were married in 1856, but there was no record of any civil or religious ceremony taking place, and she had no witness except her mother. Maggie filed several lawsuits in an effort to gain Kane's estate, but her flimsy claim couldn't convince any court to side with her.

Katie Fox never achieved her sister Maggie's level of fame. However, her activities bear review. Beyond what has already been presented about her, there are several illuminating items worth exploring.

After receiving her schooling, which Horace Greeley paid for, the "small, thin, very intelligent" woman, who enjoyed hosting séances, returned to her act. She usually, but not always, performed with Leah.

Katie was a convincing medium. Benjamin Coleman, a tireless worker for the Spiritualist cult, participated in a private séance hosted by Katie in New York, and she enthralled him.

Cromwell F. Varney, the electrician who laid the transatlantic cable, gave a lecture in 1869 to the London Dialectical Society concerning several of the electrical experiments – presumably successful – he made with Katie.

After she and Leah had convinced Charles Livermore that he had communicated with his late wife, he offered to take Katie to England with him, and with Leah's apparent blessing, she agreed. Livermore was not only a true believer, but he also promoted the Spiritualist religion. His vision was to make Katie the world's greatest Spiritualist missionary. He believed Katie could and would spread and solidify the faith.

Livermore and Katie arrived in London in 1871. He treated her in the style such a great prophet deserved. He encouraged her to live well, and he paid her lavish expenses. He even provided her with a personal servant and arranged for her to hold lucrative "professional sittings."

Livermore, however, attempted to control Katie as Leah had. He told her to "choose only those sitters who are not afraid to have their names published in confirmation of the facts they have witnessed." He also attempted to prevent any contrary views from being expressed about her performances. His efforts in this regard were geared to avoid "the irritation arising from the suspicion of skeptics."

Katie had hardly arrived in England before she was trotted out to give private performances. She held her first show on November 24, 1871. Noted Spiritualist charlatan, Daniel Dunglas Home, aided her. As often happened during seances, Katie invited an "unbiased" reporter to stand beside her and hold her hand as she called upon the dead to communicate with her. It was no surprise when the enamored reporter discovered no tricks during the séance.

Some of the other Spiritualists who attested to Katie's powers were William Crookes, Samuel Carter Hall, W. H. Harrison (editor of the *Spiritualist*), Rosamund DaleOwen who married Spiritualist Laurence Oliphant, and Reverend John Page Hopps. Naturally, it surprised no one that Spiritualists would stand with Katie.

In England, Katie's performances produced "raps (often of great power), spirit lights, direct writing, and the appearance of materialized hands." "Full form materializations" were not part of her act, however. To accomplish that, she would have needed another trickster to prance around the room with phosphorus powder sprinkled over her. Interestingly, some of the Spiritualists attending her séances did report the presence of "phosphorescent material and illumined crystals."

Noted professor and physicist William Crookes never met a Spiritualist he didn't like. He gave a glowing account of one session he had with Katie: "I was holding the medium's two hands in one of mine, while her feet were resting on my feet. Paper was on the table before us, and my disengaged hand was holding a pencil.

"A luminous hand came down from the upper part of the room, and after hovering near me for a few seconds, took the pencil from my hand, rapidly wrote on a sheet of paper, threw the pencil down, and then rose over our heads, gradually fading into darkness."

What Crookes didn't say was that in order for him to hold Katie's hands in one of his, and for her feet to be on top of his feet, she would have had to be sitting in his lap. If the pretty young maiden were sitting in his lap, it is certain that Crookes would have been, at the very least, distracted. One of the claims made by Harry Houdini and other skeptics was that mediums often used their feminine wiles to distract middle-aged men at séances. The story told by Crookes seems to confirm this.

Another interesting point about the story Crookes told is that he didn't bother to relate what the spirit wrote. Why not?

Stories were that the raps of spirits were with Katie all the time. Visitors to her home could hear them, as could people who walked along the street near her home. One could presume that she had made the raps for so long, and so often, that she could no longer control the sounds her joints made. However, the Spiritualists weren't about to consider anything that might challenge their faith.

Oddly, soon after Katie arrived in England, she met and wed H. D. Jencken. Jencken was a prominent legal scholar and "one of the earliest Spiritualists in England." The wedding took place on December 14, 1872, and the *Spiritualist* reported that ghosts "took part in the proceedings, for at the wedding breakfast loud raps were heard coming from various parts of the room, and the large table on which stood the wedding-cake was repeatedly raised from the floor."

During a séance on the first anniversary of her marriage, a spirit was supposed to have messaged Katie with the following sentence: "When shadows fall upon you, think of the brighter side." The message was later seen as a prophecy of her death. However, she lived for many years after receiving the message.

Although she was a wife and mother, Katie continued to keep up a busy schedule and made numerous performances. Professor Aleksandr Butlerov of the University of St. Petersburg was a proponent and practitioner of Spiritualism. In February 1876, Butlerov wrote in the *Spiritualist* that Katie's performances were "convincing."

Katie's husband encouraged her. He even claimed to witness many things that he said could only be performed by supernatural forces.

Jencken stated that he had witnessed a baby grand piano in his home rise a foot and a half off the floor and remain suspended for two or three minutes. He added that on several occasions spirits spelled out messages by loud raps, and tilting the piano accompanied by loud raps. Jencken said no one was near the piano when the spirit moved it.

Jencken claimed he had witnessed a table lifted one foot off the floor with no one "touching or near it at the time." He said an unnamed friend was seated on carpet and could also testify that the table rose.

Jencken said that on another occasion he saw a table lifted six feet off the ground, and an accordion was suspended off the ground for ten to twenty minutes, during which time, a spirit played it.

Jencken also stated that the most remarkable instance of a spiritual communication was at the house of James Mamby Gully. Gully's son, William Court Gully, would later become the Speaker of the British House of Commons.

Katie's husband said he once heard "three voices (no visible agencies being present) chanting a hymn accompanied by music played on an accordion suspended in the air, eight or nine feet off the ground."

It isn't certain if Katie's husband was a part of the hoax, or if he was blinded by his faith in the Spiritualist cult and by his love for his wife.

Maggie wanted desperately to break Leah's hold over her. In 1876, Maggie was penniless, friendless, and lonely. Somehow, she was able to sneak away from Leah, climb aboard a ship, and sail to Great Britain. When Maggie arrived in England, Katie welcomed her. Maggie lived with Katie and barrister Jencken for several years.

Being separated from Maggie by a wide ocean didn't dissuade Leah. Even from three thousand miles away, the eldest sister attempted to keep Maggie in the clutches of her tentacles. When Maggie resisted, Leah threatened her in every way she could imagine.

Then, when Katie's husband died in 1881, Leah went after her other sister as well. Leah went as far as to have Katie arrested, and then she filed a lawsuit to have Katie's sons taken from her. However, Katie would not give in to her manipulative older sister, and the attempt to steal the children and then trade them for Maggie failed.

Katie pointed to the incident as an example of Leah's cruelty, "She was the one who caused my arrest ... and the bringing of the preposterous charge that I was cruel to my children. I don't know why it is she has always been jealous of Maggie and me; I suppose because we could do things in Spiritualism that she couldn't."

Her husband died in 1881, leaving Katie a widow with two young sons. Soon thereafter, Spiritualists proclaimed that her children possessed "wonderful mediumship," but the boys never gained the notoriety of their mother.

After her husband's death, Katie continued her performances. Samuel Carter Hall was the Chairman of the British National Association of Spiritualists. May 9, 1882, was Hall's birthday, and he had Katie at his home to conduct a séance that evening. He was desperate to communicate with his late wife. A few days earlier, Katie had told Hall that his wife wanted to give him a birthday present.

At the beginning of the séance, a supposed message from the spirit world ordered that the lights be doused. Then, the alleged spirit of his wife took up an accordion near Hall and serenaded her husband. But the supposed ghost didn't stop there. Using Katie's hand, the ghost wrote, "I have brought you a token of love." Then, there appeared a bouquet of heartsease flowers. Hall was certain that the flowers had come from his wife. He felt the fact that he had received flowers of the same variety that morning was a mere coincidence.

9. Maggie and Katie Confess

MAGGIE Fox felt guilty for her part in the fraud from almost the outset. In late 1850, or early 1851, she admitted to Vernelia Culver that she was afraid of her older sister, that she was a fraud, and that she had faked the rapping sounds. Before then, Mrs. Culver had believed the girls were communicating with the spirit world. Maggie told Mrs. Culver that she created the rapping sounds by snapping her toes, knees, and ankles.

Culver signed a statement on April 17, 1851, witnessed by a doctor and a clergyman. The statement related what Culver said Maggie told her. The statement was published in the *New York World*.

Additionally, Culver admitted that she had helped Katie and Maggie during their act. She said she touched them to let them know when and how to rap.

Culver stated that Katie even taught her how to make the rapping sounds. With some practice, Culver became fairly good at making the sounds from the beyond. She found it was easier to make the rapping if her feet were "thoroughly warmed."

Katie, according to Culver, also taught her "how to manage to answer the questions" posed to the supposed spirits. Katie said it was easy to answer correctly if the person asking the question called out letters of the alphabet. They would have the people they were tricking place several names on paper, then they'd rap out letters of the alphabet until they matched one of the names. They would watch the reaction of the people they were tricking, and that way they could almost always make the right guess.

Culver proved to be a wealth of information about how the fraud took place. She said Katie showed her how they held down and moved tables. She said all one had to do was to put one's foot on the bottom of the table when making the rapping sound with her foot. If one wanted to make it appear that the rapping was coming from a distant wall, all she had to do was make the rapping louder, and to stare at the wall. People would trick themselves into believing that the sound was coming from there.

Katie demonstrated to Culver that if she put her foot against the bottom of a door and rapped, the sound would be heard at the top of the door. Katie also showed Culver the trick of making sounds that resembled saws cutting wood.

Culver continued that Katie told her how they passed the tests they were given by skeptics in Rochester. When their ankles were held in place, a "Dutch servant girl rapped with her knuckles under the floor from the cellar." The Dutch girl was instructed to rap every time she heard the girls calling the spirits.

According to Culver, while she was in Rochester, Maggie told her that when skeptics insisted upon seeing her feet and toes during her performances, she simply used her knee and ankle to make raps.

How did the girls gain their "incredible" powers? Culver said that Katie told her that her sister was "playing with her toes against the footboard when in bed" one night when she discovered her talent to make rapping sounds.

The apologists for Spiritualism challenged Culver's statement by denying that a Dutch servant had helped the girls. They also said that Katie was elsewhere when the tests at Rochester were conducted in November 1849. What the Spiritualists didn't do was present anything amounting to proof that the rapping could not be produced as Katie said it was.

Vernelia Culver's statement did nothing to slow the growth of the Spiritualist cult. The true believers either branded Culver a liar or they simply ignored her statement. The faithful Spiritualists hurried to state that even though Culver provided several physical examples of how the Fox girls performed their parlor tricks, she didn't produce proof positive that the girls were fakes. After all, they reasoned, the girls had never been caught in the act of flimflamming their audiences.

Besides that, the apologists for the Spiritualists pointed to the fact that Culver admitted that she had taken part in faking contact with the dead. The Spiritualists asked if Culver would deceive before, why wouldn't she attempt to deceive now?

What the spiritualists didn't think about was that if they believed that Culver had faked contact with the dead, it meant that the Fox girls were fakes too.

The Culver confession faded from the public mind quickly. However, Spiritualism faced a more serious problem during the autumntime of 1888. After four decades of being the poster children for Spiritualism, the Fox girls, now both middle-aged and widowed, confessed independently of one another that they were frauds. Maggie even demonstrated before large audiences how she used her toe joints in her early performances.

But why wait so long to confess? The truth is, as stated in the paragraphs above, the girls had revealed the hoax years before. But there are reasons why they confessed again in 1888.

First, Maggie was devastated by the death of her husband in 1857. Then after she was unable to gain any of her husband's wealth, she was morose, and without money or friends.

With no other options, the bitter woman returned to the Spiritualist performance circuit. She traveled about the country trying to eke out a modest living while remaining under Leah's thumb until 1876, when she joined her sister Katie in England.

Maggie felt she had been forced "into hell" by the hoax. In her agony, Maggie continued her heavy drinking, which only added to her troubles.

For years, Maggie had wanted to confess that she was a fraud. However, even while she was in England, she feared her sister Leah to the degree that she dared not to speak out. But after time, Maggie's newly adopted Christian faith gave her the courage to finally reveal the hoax. Upon her arrival back in New York, Maggie signed a confession which was delivered to the press on October 21, 1888.

She wrote why she finally revealed the Spiritualism hoax. She suffered from extreme guilt, and she had health issues as well. She said later that she came to "loathe the thing I have been. I have seen so much miserable deception! Every morning of my life I have it before me. When I wake up, I brood over it. That is why I am willing to state that Spiritualism is a fraud of the worst description. I have had a life of sorrow ... but I consider it my duty, a sacred thing, a holy mission to expose it.

"I want to see the day when it is entirely done away with." She then added that if she wasn't successful in destroying Spiritualism, "At least I hope to reduce the ranks of the eight million Spiritualists in the country. I go into it as into a holy war."

She said that while she had joined the Catholic church, no one within the church "has advised me to make these public exposures and confession. It is my own idea. My own mission. I would have done it long ago if I could have had the necessary money and courage to do it. I could not find anyone to help me – I was too timid to ask."

Maggie stated that she was "waiting anxiously and fearlessly for the moment" when she could put on demonstrations and prove that "all Spiritualism is a fraud and a deception ... a branch of legerdemain."

Then Maggie proceeded to tell her story in detail. She reminded the public that she and Katie were children when their horrible deception started.

But how did it begin?

Maggie said she and her sister were "very mischievous children and sought merely to terrify our dear mother, who was a very good woman and very easily frightened."

Maggie explained that when she and Katie went to bed at night, they'd tie an apple to a string and move the string up and down, causing the apple to bump on the floor. Or they would drop the apple on the floor and it would make a "strange noise every time it would rebound."

Maggie said her mother was frightened by the sound and that she never suspected the girls of tricking her because they were so young. Maggie continued that after a few nights, her mother couldn't stand the strange sounds any longer. Margaret Fox felt compelled to tell the neighbors about the sounds. Invariably, she asked her neighbors, "Is this a disembodied spirit that has taken possession of my dear children?" Several of the neighbors thought it was.

Here Maggie contradicted what her mother said in early April 1848. Mrs. Fox said she didn't contact the neighbors until March 31. According to Maggie, the neighbors had been visiting for days before March 31.

With so many people coming to the house to witness the strange sounds, Maggie and Katie worried that they'd be found out. She said at first she and Katie were having fun at the expense of their parents and their neighbors, but after a while they feared that if they stopped, they'd endure severe punishment.

The girls decided that they didn't want to abandon their trickery. They couldn't perform their apple trick except when they were in bed and the room was dark. Along with the apple trick, they could sometimes fool people by rapping on the bedstead, but it was dangerous because the chances of being detected were high.

The girls soon found another method of fooling the gullible of the Hydesville hamlet. Maggie stated that she and her sister made "a most wonderful discovery, a very wonderful thing" which allowed them to continue their mischief. They could make rapping sounds with their toes.

From the beginning, the neighbors were convinced that someone had been murdered in the house, and the girls confirmed it with one rap from the great beyond, not the three raps that they would answer with later.

The Fox girls, so said Maggie, didn't identify Mr. Bell as the murderer. She said that the neighbors scoured the "whole surrounding country" gathering the names of previous residents of the Fox house. Finally, the witch hunt by the good people of Hydesville led them to Mr. Bell. They declared that he was the murderer, and that the spirit of the victim was haunting the Fox house. The whole community shunned Bell, and he never convinced them of his innocence.

Oddly, Leah had previously mentioned that she and Maggie sometimes played tricks on their mother, even after they became well known to the Spiritualist community. In these instances, they pretended to raise spirits by the use of trickery. "Maggie went into the parlor bedroom, and I laid down on the sofa. She took a cane and I a shell from the table to rap with."

Maggie recounted how Leah took the girls to Rochester where they performed and devised new ways to make the rapping sounds. She said, "Katie was the first to observe that by swishing her fingers she could produce certain noises with her knuckles and joints" which sounded the same as the sounds they made with their toes. Then they found new ways to rap with their feet, first with one foot and then with both."

The tricks required considerable skill, and they weren't easy to perform. Maggie revealed that she and Katie practiced for hours until they could make the sounds easily, even in a dark room.

Leah was a major component of the act. Maggie related, "To all questions we answered by raps, we knew when to rap 'yes' or 'no' according to certain signs which [Leah] gave us during the séance."

The methods Maggie described matched what the doctors in Buffalo had discovered many years earlier. While the sisters survived that investigation without being completely discredited, they knew they were in constant danger of being exposed. Maggie wrote, "as the world grew wise and science began to investigate we began to adapt our experiments to our audiences. Our séances were held in a room with a center-table in the middle and we all stood around it."

Maggie added that a big part of their con job was reading the people at the séances. She said they would "watch minutely the faces of sitters." Then they would gear their performance to the changes in the expressions of those they were bilking.

Maggie placed most of the blame for the growth of Spiritualism on her sister Leah, and rightly so. Maggie said she owed all her misfortune to Leah. Even after Leah married David Underhill and became wealthy, she still wouldn't let Maggie confess.

Maggie tried several times to get Leah to admit the hoax and "save her soul," but whenever she did, Leah "would fly into a passion." Maggie said Leah "wanted to establish a new religion and she told me that she received messages from spirits. She knew that we were tricking people, but she tried to make us believe spirits existed. She told us that before we were born spirits came into her room and told her that we were destined for great things."

Maggie's confession was published in *New York World* on October 21, 1888. That evening she was scheduled to appear at the Academy of Music in New York and demonstrate how she produced the rapping sounds.

There were fears that some of the Spiritualist mediums whose livelihood might be threatened by Maggie would try to "kidnap" her. The day of her public demonstration, she was guarded heavily. Additionally, while Maggie waited out the day, she agreed to be interviewed by reporters. She had only expected to answer questions, but when one journalist asked her to show him "how the trick was done," she agreed to demonstrate it.

The reporter stated that the private demonstration went like this:

Maggie said, "I will stand up before these folding-doors and you may stand as near as you please and I will call up any 'spirit' that you wish and answer any questions. One rap means 'no' and three raps mean 'yes.' Are you ready?"

The reporter nodded and asked, "Is Napoleon Bonaparte present?"

He was watching Maggie closely, but he didn't see her do anything to cause the three raps he heard.

The reporter's next asked, "Does he know me? I mean, did he ever meet and converse with me?"

There were three raps in answer.

Maggie smiled and asked the reporter, "That is strange, isn't it, in view of the fact that he must have died before you were born?"

The reporter next asked, "Is Abraham Lincoln present?"

There were three raps from the dead President.

Still smiling, Maggie told the reporter, "'Well you see the 'spirits' are very obliging."

The reporter inquired, "Will Harrison be elected?"

One loud rap answered with an emphatic, "No."

The reporter followed with, "Will President Cleveland get another term?"

Three raps answered in the affirmative.

Just for the record, Harrison was elected.

Finally, after her long day with the reporters, Maggie was seated in a buggy and transported to the Academy of Music where more than 2,000 interested people crammed into the hall in anticipation of her announcement that she, and the Spiritualist cult, were fraudulent.

The composition of this audience in the hall was somewhat different from the true believers Maggie usually performed before. A majority of the people there were skeptics who looked forward to Maggie making a "clean breast of her share in Spiritualistic humbuggery." However, there were hundreds of Spiritualists there as well, and they felt personally insulted by efforts to prove their cult was based on a hoax.

The exhibition opened with Dr. C. M. Richmond putting on a demonstration. The New York dentist had been investigating Spiritualism for two decades. He had also spent thousands of dollars exposing the tricks performed by mediums. Richmond explained calmly how the performers fooled people. Then, with the lights shining brightly, he demonstrated some of the methods employed by the con artists in darkness or dim light.

The true believers in the audience hurled profanities at Richmond, and it appeared they might become violent. However, guards were present and no one dared rush the stage.

When Dr. Richmond finished, Maggie took center stage and was greeted by a mixture of cheers and hisses. She was ready to "confess orally what she had already confessed in print." However, her emotion was so great that she couldn't deliver a speech to the audience. Instead, she went straight into a demonstration.

She had a plain, four-legged wooden table placed in front of her. She took off her right shoe and placed her bare foot upon the table. The previously unruly crowd became utterly silent as they awaited Maggie's attempt to replicate the weird and mysterious sounds that had befuddled hundreds of thousands of Americans and Europeans for forty years. Maggie made a slight movement of her big toe and a number of raps could be heard throughout the hall.

Then a committee of three doctors came out of the audience and examined the big toe on Maggie's right foot. They all agreed that the rapping was coming from the first joint of the said toe.

Maggie's demonstration was utterly convincing. However, the true believers were so deluded that even if their opinion of Maggie had changed, their opinion of their Spiritualist cult had not. They went home that night still convinced that there was a spiritual world, and that it could be contacted.

Katie had traveled to New York, and although she didn't take part in it, she attended Maggie's demonstration. Afterward, Katie admitted her part in the hoax and she told the world that Spiritualism was "all humbuggery, every bit of it."

Naturally, the public confessions drew massive attention. The doubters felt justified in their skepticism. Many, perhaps most, felt that the Spiritualist cult was floating dead face first in the ocean of truth.

But faith dies hard and most true believers refused to accept Maggie's confession. Moreover, there was another group of Spiritualists who held that even if Maggie was a fraud, their religion was not. This class of Spiritualists believed that it was important to expose the few con artists in the community to keep the religion pure and free of deception. These men and women chose to forget – or ignore – the fact that their entire religion was built upon the shaky ground of the rapping sounds which Maggie had just proven were of the human realm.

Years later, Harry Houdini stated his belief that Maggie's confession had forever hobbled Spiritualism. He wrote that the Spiritualists could deny the examinations by the doctors in Buffalo, and the statement given by Vernelia

Culver, but he added, "I have yet to meet a representative of theirs who can plausibly explain away what happened in 1888."

Some Spiritualists expressed bewilderment and confusion in their letters to Maggie. A Spiritualist from San Franciso wrote:

"I have been a believer in the phenomena from its first inception through you and your sister, believing it to be true since that time.

"I am now eighty-one years old and have but a short time of course, to remain in this world, and I feel a great anxiety to know through you if I have been deceived all this time in a matter of vital interest to us all."

A letter from a disillusioned Spiritualist from Boston read: "Hundreds of thousands have believed through you and you alone. Hundreds of thousands eagerly ask you whether all the glorious light that they fancied you had given them, was but the false flicker of a common dip-candle of fraud?

"If, as you say, you were forced to pursue this imposture from childhood, I can forgive you, and I am sure God will; for he turns not back the truly repentant. I will not upbraid you. I am sure you have suffered as much as any penalty, human or divine, could cause you to suffer. The disclosures that you make take from me all that I have cherished most. There is nothing left for me now but to hope for the reality of that repose which death promises us.

"It is perhaps better that the delusion should be at last swept away by one single word, and that word is 'fraud.'

"I know that the pursuit of this shadowy belief has wrought upon my brain and that I am no longer my old self. Money I have spent in thousands and thousands of dollars within a few short years to propitiate the 'mediumistic' intelligence. It is true that never once have I received a message or the token of a word that did not leave a still unsatisfied longing in my heart, a feeling that it was not really my loved one after all who was speaking to me, or if it was my loved one that he was changed, that I hardly knew him and he hardly knew me. But that must have been the true intuition. It is better that the delusion is past, after all, for had I kept on in that way, I am sure I should have gone mad. The constant seeking, the frequent pretended response, its unsatisfying meaning, the sense of distance and change between me and my loved one—oh! It has been horrible, horrible!

"He who is dying of thirst and has the sweet cup ever snatched from his lips, just as the first drop touches them – he alone can know what in actual things is the similitude of this Spiritualistic torture.

"God bless you, for I think that you now speak the truth. You have my forgiveness at least, and I believe that thousands of others will forgive you, for the atonement made in season wipes out much of the stain of the early sin."

Maggie made it clear that neither she nor Katie ever thought about spirits or bringing them from the beyond. She said, "I know that there is no such thing as the departed returning to this life. Many people have said to me that such a thing was possible and seemed to believe so firmly in it that I tried to see, and I have tried in every form and know that it cannot be done."

So why did she continue with the hoax?

Maggie reminded those interested that she had given up her shows while she was married, but when he died he left her with nothing. Having no other means of income, Maggie felt driven to resume performing.

Decades after Maggie and Katie confessed, Sir Arthur Conan Doyle was still trying to control the damage they caused. He told Spiritualists that the confessions "are not to be taken too seriously." However, he took them very seriously. In fact, the great English novelist took the confessions so seriously that he was willing to spin a fictional yarn to disprove them.

Doyle had no concrete evidence with which to discredit the confessions, so he sought to discredit Maggie and Katie as individuals. He besmirched their characters by claiming the two younger sisters had confessed because of their hatred of Leah. He continued that they were motivated by money.

Doyle reserved his greatest criticism for Maggie. Ironically, the most fanatical Spiritualist on earth attacked Maggie for her alleged "religious fanaticism." He charged that she had been turned against Spiritualism by the leaders of the "Church of Rome." Doyle pointed to Cardinal Henry Edward Manning as the church leader most responsible for influencing her and convincing her that her powers were evil.

Doyle had never been a Christian, and it isn't surprising that he would blame Christianity for Maggie's confession. But one must admit that associating Cardinal Manning with Maggie was clever. Manning, who left the Anglican Church and became a Catholic, remains a controversial figure even to this day. Doyle, it seems, hoped that by tying Maggie to Manning it would further damage her reputation.

Doyle's mudslinging didn't stop there. He declared that at the time of her confession, Maggie was "near madness," and that she "broke out into absolute raving against her older sister." Doyle then continued to disparage Maggie by calling her an "unbalanced woman, acting not only from motives of hatred but also from ... the hope of pecuniary reward."

Doyle even went as far as circulating the never-proven rumor that Maggie was paid $1,500 to demonstrate how she deceived the gullible Spiritualists.

Doyle's hypocrisy and dishonesty was amazing. Evidently, he believed that the Spiritualists wouldn't bother to read Maggie's confession. That made him feel comfortable mischaracterizing it. There was no "absolute raving" in the confession. Considering the abuse she had suffered at Leah's hands for 40 years, Maggie was remarkably restrained.

Doyle definitely knew that from March 31, 1848, through forty years later, when the Fox sisters confessed, Spiritualists had supported them financially. He also knew that the Spiritualists would have rewarded Maggie and Katie handsomely to remain silent. His repeating the rumors that Maggie's public confession may have netted her $1,500 proved nothing. The fact remained that Maggie had proven she had faked her communications with spirits. Whether or not she was paid didn't matter.

Doyle had no reasonable explanation for the fact that Maggie had shown publicly how she and her sisters performed their tricks. Apparently without sensing the irony, he accused her of faking the rapping sounds she produced during her confession. He stated that "in so large a hall any prearranged sound might be attributed to the medium." It seemed to never occur to him that the same thing could have been said for any of the hundreds of performances that he declared were real.

Doyle tried to explain away why the Fox girls may have sometimes resorted to cheating. He also suggested a remedy to prevent other mystics from committing fraud in the future.

Doyle wrote that the "dangers lie in the weakening of the will, in the extreme debility after phenomenal sittings, ... in the temptation to fraud ..." He then offered, "The remedy is to segregate mediums, to give them salaries instead of paying them by results, to regulate the number of their sittings and the character of the sitters, and thus to remove them from influences which overwhelmed the Fox sisters as they have done other of the strongest mediums in the past."

Doyle's dedication to the Spiritualist cult are explored in greater detail in Chapter 11.

10. Maggie and Katie Recant

MAGGIE'S plan after her confession was to earn her living giving lectures exposing the hoax that was Spiritualism. She also assumed that she could rely on the moral support from the community of skeptics. She was disappointed on both fronts.

While hundreds – sometimes thousands – had turned out to watch her do her tricks, few were interested in hearing the soft-spoken Maggie give a lecture. The Spiritualists had held her up as a shining light for the world to see, but the skeptics didn't need a poster child to convince anyone that Spiritualism was phony. Neither did they see reason to coddle the discredited medium. Before long, Maggie was down and out again.

Maggie's confession in the brightly lit and crowded theatre where she deliberately revealed the method of making the raps which had brought her fame for four decades had negligible impact. She soon realized that she had changed few, if any, minds. Unable to overcome the demon of alcoholism, and totally destitute, Maggie was forced back into the clutches of the cult she had attempted to disown.

The poor woman endured a great deal of pressure from the President of the First Society of Spiritualists, and he apparently convinced her that it would be in her best interest, and the best interest of Spiritualism, for her to back away from her confession.

Maggie's only skill was tricking the credulous, and she saw no alternative except to return to it. Her first step was to disown previous statements. On November 20, 1889, a newspaper printed an interview with Maggie in which she recanted her confession.

She told the reporter that her confession was "false in every particular." She said her faith in Spiritualism had not undergone any change. She continued: "When I made those dreadful statements, I was not responsible for my words." She explained, "At that time I was in great need of money, and persons ... took advantage of the situation, hence the trouble. The excitement, too, helped to upset my mental equilibrium."

She was asked what the motives of the people who convinced her to confess were. She answered, "They had several objects in view. Their first and paramount idea was to crush Spiritualism, to make money for themselves, and to get up a great excitement, as that was an element in which they flourish."

In a rare moment of candor, Maggie admitted to the reporter that she intended to profit from her recantation. She said, "You know that even a mortal instrument in the hands of the spirit must have the maintenance of life. This I propose to derive from my lectures."

However, Maggie told the reporter that she wouldn't hold séances in the future. She said, "I will devote myself entirely to platform work, as that will find me a better opportunity to refute the foul slanders uttered by me against Spiritualism."

When asked if she'd have an agent to book her performances, Maggie responded, "No, sir. I have a horror of them. They, too, treated me most outrageously. Frank Stecher acted shamefully with me. He made considerable money through his management for me, and left me in Boston without a cent. All I got from him was $550, which was given to me at the beginning of the contract." She didn't mention the fact that her sister Leah had robbed her.

Despite saying she wouldn't, Maggie began holding private séances and public performances across the United States. However, she never again saw the kinds of crowds she had seen in previous years. Instead of the thousands who had flocked to see her performances, only a smattering of people were willing to purchase tickets to her shows. It was apparent that her confession of deceit made it difficult for her to fool the public again.

Only a few unshakable Spiritualists came to see Maggie repeat the same old routine that she had been performing since her youth. These Spiritualists couldn't believe she was a fraud. Most didn't believe that her confession was a lie either. They seemed certain that she "had fallen into the hands of evil spirits when she confessed that she was a fraud."

Maggie said that Katie was in complete sympathy for her. Maggie continued that Katie hadn't approved of the original confession to begin with.

It is true that Katie agreed with Maggie's embracement of Spiritualism again, but Katie had supported Maggie's original confession too. However, Katie didn't go before the public and say anything either way in 1889.

Speculation was that Leah had pressured Katie to go back on her confession, but neither she nor Katie said so. It is more likely that Katie was merely trying to help her indigent sister by recanting herself. However, that can't be proven.

11. The High Priest of Spiritualism

WHILE there were – and are – many, many apologists for the Spiritualist cult, Sir Arthur Conan Doyle holds the distinction as being the cult's most famous and greatest evangelist.

A doctor by trade, who also had a law degree, Doyle was a great storyteller. He gained world renown with his first Sherlock Holmes novel in 1887. He followed that with three other Holmes novels and 56 short stories featuring the fictional detective. Doyle also wrote a variety of other novels and stories, but it is the great deductive powers he displayed through Sherlock Holmes that gave him lasting fame.

There was no greater Spiritualist believer than Doyle. Even though he had proven his amazing analytical ability and critical thinking in the Sherlock Holmes stories, when it came to Spiritualism, he had an enormous blind spot. He began "investigating" the movement in 1887. He attended some twenty seances, witnessed experiments in telepathy, and had private sittings with mediums. Before the end of the year, his doubts had evaporated, and he had become a devout Spiritualist.

In 1889, he helped found the Hampshire Society for Psychical Research, and in 1893, he joined the National Society for Psychical Research in London.

The great novelist traveled throughout much of the English-speaking world and gave lectures to thousands of true believers promoting his religion. He also engaged in contentious debates with the world-famous magician Harry Houndini, and the skeptic Joseph McCabe.

While sparring with his skeptical opponents, Doyle readily admitted that there were charlatans operating in the Spiritualist movement. He referred to the Spiritualist con artists as "hyenas." However, he could not see through the Fox sisters, or most others that claimed to be in contact with the world of spirits. In fact, he said their ability to call the dead was "the same power which is used by the Buddha and by the Woman of Endor."

The "Woman of Endor" which Doyle mentioned as a medium is better known as the "Witch of Endor." According to some interpretations of the

Old Testament book of *First Samuel*, King Saul forced the Witch of Endor to summon the spirit of the prophet of Samuel.

In 1919, the mustachioed Englishman expressed his faith when he wrote, that "when the young Fox girl struck her hands together and cried 'Do as I do' ... it was, as time will more and more clearly show, one of the turning points of the world's history, greater far than the fall of thrones or the rout of armies."

By 1920, the Fox sisters had been dead for decades and their fakery was widely known. It was about this time that Doyle conceded, "I am prepared even to admit that, amid much conflicting testimony and complications, the record of the Fox sisters leaves a suspicion that their strong and undoubted powers may finally have been artificially aided."

A close reading of Doyle's statement indicates that he in no way repudiated the three Fox sisters. He held that they possessed "undoubted powers" which "may" have been "artificially aided." He evidently believed that the Fox sisters were honest at first, and only later, when under severe pressure to achieve results, they might they have turned to cheating.

Then, in 1921, Doyle tried to separate the humbug practiced by the girls from their gifts. He wrote that "the actual character of a man is as much separate from his mediumistic powers, as it would be from his musical powers. Both are inborn gifts beyond the control of their possessor. The medium is the telegraph instrument and the telegraph boy united in one, but the real power is that which transmits the message, which he only receives and delivers. The remark applies to the Fox sisters ..."

In 1923, Doyle was still defending the Fox girls. He wrote, "Any theory that the phenomena were caused by mischievous children becomes untenable when measured by the actual facts."

Neither Spiritualist true believers nor Doyle ever disowned the Fox sisters – not even Leah. In 1923, Doyle happily related that on a trip to the National Spiritualist Association headquarters in Washington, D. C., he saw several "remarkable pictures of the three Fox sisters" displayed there.

Doyle continued his defense of the "poor Fox girls." He wrote, "The time is coming when a tardy justice will be done to their memory ... and all the other persecuted exponents of the humble but necessary physical signs."

Doyle had little respect for the Unites States. Yet, he was so enamored with the cult sparked by the Fox girls that he stated Spiritualism was "the most important thing which ever came out of" America.

Doyle felt it was a disgrace that city leaders in Rochester hadn't erected a monument for the Fox girls. This was because he believed that Rochester, not Hydesville, was the Mecca of Spiritualism. The great novelist stated flatly that their Rochester performances were "so final in their proofs of independent intelligence, amazed the populace, and aroused those murderous passions which every fresh psychic development, from the time of Jesus, has stirred to fury."

It is interesting that Doyle would choose to invoke the name of Jesus. Spiritualism isn't a Christian sect, and Doyle had never been a Christian. He wrote that before he became a Spiritualist, "I did not, of course, believe in an anthropomorphic God, but I believed then, as I believe now, in an intelligent Force behind, all the operations of Nature ... but when it came to a question of our little personalities surviving death, it seemed to me that the whole analogy of Nature was against it."

Doyle would sometimes fudge the truth in defense of his faith. He stated that while at Rochester, the Fox girls "were summoned before three meetings at the Corinthian Hall and were forced to show their powers, each meeting ending by the appointment of a Committee of Examination. Each Committee in turn was forced to admit the reality of the phenomena." Doyle's statement was not true. Those examining the shows generally branded the girls as frauds.

In 1926, Doyle once again contended that the rapping sounds in the Fox house were genuine. He said, "Just such raps ... had occurred in England in 1661 ... at Oppenheim, in Germany, in 1520, and ... the Epworth Vicarage in 1716." Doyle was certain the strange noises scattered across the earth over three centuries were somehow related, and rapping sounds in Germany in 1520 somehow proved that spirits were communicating with the Fox girls in 1848.

The British novelist seemed to have forgotten that the Fox girls had allegedly communicated with a man who had been murdered in 1844. How he connected that spirit with a spirit from two centuries before was never established.

Doyle bragged that as interest in the spirits grew, they became more active. It never occurred to him that the girls, or rather, those controlling the girls, increased the frequency of their séances as they became more famous. The increase helped them to cash in on the gullible true believers.

Doyle repeated with sincerity that during the night of March 31, a neighbor took the girls home with her, and their mother spent the night with a neighbor woman named Redfield. Doyle continued: "In their absence the phenomena went on exactly the same as before, which disposes once for all of those theories of cracking toes and dislocating knees which have been so frequently put forward by people unaware of the true facts."

Doyle's "true facts" caused a thorny problem for him and other Spiritualists. If the girls were true mediums, and the spirit worked through them, when they were removed from the house, it would have stopped. On the other hand, if the spirit didn't work through the girls, they weren't mediums, and their later performances were all faked.

Doyle tried to rationalize the contradiction away. He held that the girls were mediums, and that the spirit "seemed to have permeated the house and to have been at the disposal of the manifesting power" even when the girls weren't present there. Doyle eventually contended nonsensically that after a time, "these unseen forces were no longer attached to any building, but that they had transferred themselves to the girls."

Another inconsistency in the story Doyle told about March 31, was that the ghost rapped out his name "Charles B. Rosma." However, Duesler stated that only the letters "C. R." were rapped out. Given the massive publicity the case generated, if a peddler by the name of Charles B. Rosma had visited Hydesville, why, if he was alive, wasn't he ever located? And if he was dead, why did no one ever locate his family members?

Doyle had an explanation for this prickly problem, too. He wrote, "we appreciate how very difficult it is to get names correctly across. A name apparently is a purely conventional thing, and as such very different from an idea. Every practicing Spiritualist has received messages which were correct coupled with names which were mistaken. It is possible that the real name was Ross, or possibly Rosmer, and that this error prevented identification."

Even for Doyle, the explanation that the peddler was never located because his spirit couldn't spell was weak.

Additionally, Doyle stated that while digging in the cellar, David Fox and the others "found "human hair and bones, which were pronounced by expert medical testimony to belong to a human skeleton." In truth, no such "medical testimony" was ever given.

Doyle didn't have an explanation as to why the spirit didn't know "his body had been moved from the center of the cellar to the wall, where it was eventually found."

It is unknown where Doyle got his information, but it is hard to imagine how he could not have known that his information was very, very wrong.

Some of Doyle's statements about the Fox girls and their activities were flat out false. He wrote, "Every effort was made to conceal these manifestations from the public, but they soon became known." He then added, "Mrs. Fish, who was a teacher of music, was unable to continue her profession." Doyle had to know that Leah promoted the girls relentlessly, that she publicized their shows widely, and that she made huge amounts of money from their performances.

When relating that Leah also received the powers her sisters possessed, Doyle explained that the powers the girls possessed were "contagious." He also stated that Leah's powers were of a lesser degree than those of her sisters. He didn't explain how some mediums had lesser abilities than others did.

Even in the absurd, silly putty world of Spiritualism, the idea that one could "catch" clairvoyant powers from another mystic was ridiculous. The idea that mediums were of different degrees didn't make any sense either.

Doyle, it seems, refused to consider that since she was older than they were, Leah may not have had the flexibility to perform some of her sisters' tricks.

Even when Doyle was forced to admit that a Spiritualist medium was wrong, he wouldn't accuse the medium of fakery. Sir Arthur recounted an episode at Rochester shortly after the Fox girls became famous.

In July or August of 1848, a tobacco peddler in Rochester disappeared suddenly. The man had several hundred dollars on his person when he vanished, and the fear was that he had been robbed and murdered. A large reward was offered to anyone who could discern the whereabouts of the missing peddler.

Several of the many, many imitators of the Fox sisters held séances trying to identify the location of the man or his body. Finally, one self-proclaimed clairvoyant declared that he had the answer. He said the rapping sounds he heard told him that a missing man had been murdered and dumped into the nearby canal.

Local authorities searched for the peddler by dragging the identified location of the canal, but without success. The medium then stated that the peddler's body had been moved from its original location, and he provided the authorities with the new underwater resting place of the peddler.

Another search took place, but the body wasn't found in the second location the spirits had predicted. The confident medium again quoted the spirits as saying the body had been moved just ahead of the search. He then relayed that the spirits told him where the body had been resubmerged.

The canal superintendent announced it would be drained where the clairvoyant said the body's new location was. However, before the draining could begin, the spirits related to the medium that the body had been relocated once again. Based on what was conveyed to him, he promised to retrieve the body himself, with the help of his wife and their daughter. Their effort almost led to a tragedy.

In their attempt to find the body, the Spiritualist, his wife, and their twelve-year-old daughter slowly entered the chilly water at a predetermined point in the canal. Even though the spirits had forbidden her to do so, the woman tied a rope around her waist and had someone hold it, ready to pull her out in an emergency. It was a wise thing to do. The woman fell and would have surely drowned had not her ally dragged her out of the water to safety.

The little girl was also injured in the failed enterprise. She stepped on something on the bottom of the canal and suffered a severe cut to her foot.

The peddler wasn't found. The red-faced and wet Spiritualist didn't have an excuse for why he failed again. He took his injured family home, completely discredited. Naturally, city officials at long last stopped paying attention to him.

Several months passed before the mystery was solved. The alleged murder victim showed up at home very much alive. He admitted that he had skipped across the border into Canada to avoid his creditors.

An unbiased observer would have suspected that the medium in this case was a fraud, or that he may have had sinister designs, such as devising a clever scheme to murder his wife.

Sir Arthur Conan Doyle was never accused of being unbiased. He claimed the Spiritualist was honest, but that "mischievous and humorous entities" had lied to him from the outset.

Doyle had developed a theory that tricks played by mean spirits were common. He confided that he "himself had his faith sorely shaken by deception until some compensating proof has come along to assure him that it was only a lesson which he had received, and that it was no more fiendish or even remarkable that disembodied intelligences should be hoaxers than that the same intelligence inside a human body should find amusement in the same foolish way."

Naturally, if the failures of mediums could always be attributed to "mischievous and humorous entities," then it would be impossible to ever challenge any mystic. Sir Arthur didn't want to consider any challenge to any medium, so the "mischievous and humorous entities" theory fit him beautifully.

Doyle had always held traditional Christianity with disdain. He claimed that the ghosts were offended by religious leaders who refused to believe in the Fox girls. He wrote, "So incensed were the discarnate Guides by the opposition of their earthly agents that they threatened to suspend the whole movement for a generation, and did actually desert them completely for some weeks."

The indignation-filled Doyle wrote of the Christians, "The majority thundered from their pulpits against [the Fox girls], and the mob eagerly joined in the cowardly sport of heretic-baiting."

It is interesting that Doyle thought it cowardly to oppose fraud. His most famous fictional character, Sherlock Holmes, exposed several frauds in the stories Arthur penned.

Eliah W. Capron agreed that the spirits threatened to abandon Leah and her sisters, but he said it was for a different reason. According to Capron, in November 1848, the spirits demanded that unless the Fox girls agreed to continue their performances, they would "bid you all farewell" in twenty minutes. When the girls refused, the spirits went away for twelve days until the girls relented and resumed their act.

Capron's statement was pure bunk, but the alleged threat of the spirits to leave was a great excuse for the girls to continue their performances.

Doyle also had harsh words for Vernelia Culver (see Chapter 6). He called her revelation of how the Fox sisters executed their tricks "an entire fabrication." Yet, he never offered any proof that Mrs. Culver was a liar.

Despite his years of defending the Fox sisters, in 1926, Doyle stated that their powers were "to some extent at least, under their control." However, he offered an explanation as to why the sisters could have control over their powers without perpetrating a fraud. He said the rapping sounds were "caused by a protrusion from the medium's person of a long rod of a substance having certain properties which distinguish it from all other forms of matter." The "protrusions" were, according to Doyle, what French Spiritualist Charles Richet had called "ectoplasm."

Doyle presented two assumptions that he believed science would eventually prove to be correct.

First, according to his hypothesis, the force that drew the spirit to the living world was formed in some part of the human body from which the ectoplasm rod protruded. According to Doyle, such an ectoplasm rod existed in Maggie's foot, and that is where the rapping sounds emanated from. Thus, Maggie's foot was connected directly to the spirit. Doyle explained that was why the professors at Buffalo detected the movement of Maggie's foot at the same time the raps were heard.

Doyle's second assumption was that Maggie could cause the protrusion of the ectoplasmic rods at will. This was an explanation as to why she confessed. According to Doyle, Maggie knew she was causing the rapping sounds, but she didn't realize that the spirits were actually making them. Thus, he concluded that she wasn't a fraud, nor was she a liar. He thought she was simply ignorant of what was happening.

If the assumptions were correct, and Doyle was certain they were, then every time examiners had thought they had caught Maggie in an act of deception, they had in fact proven her to be a true medium.

In reviewing Doyle's contrived scientific assumptions, it must be pointed out that he made other assumptions as well. He assumed that ectoplasm rods existed. The fact that in the century since he assumed this, ectoplasm has never been found outside science fiction novels and movies tells everything that we need to know about the assumption.

Another assumption Doyle made was that Maggie, despite her statements to the contrary, wasn't a fraud. If he was correct, when Maggie revealed her tricks in front of thousands of spectators, she must have really been extracting spirits from the world of the dead, and those spirits were willing to pretend they didn't really exist.

There was another matter that Doyle had conveniently forgotten. He was on record saying that when the Fox girls were removed from their house in 1848, the murdered peddler's spirit continued his rapping rampage. How, if the spirit entered the material world through the ectoplasmic rod in Maggie's foot, could it remain in the house after she departed? Or if it did, what kept it from being trapped forever in the material world when its conduit to the spiritual realm was removed?

It is remarkable that a man of such a deep intellect as Sir Arthur Conan Doyle would abandon all his innate objectivity. He chose to stress those items regarding Spirituality that suited his purposes, even when they were outlandish, outrageous, and just plain silly. Moreover, Doyle omitted those things that didn't confirm his beliefs even when they were indisputable.

12. Ben Franklin and Other Spirits

Spiritualists were human. As such, they put more stock in the messages of dead celebrities than they did the messages that came from ordinary everyday ghosts.

According to the mediums, one of the most prolific spirits was Benjamin Franklin. There are numerous examples of Spiritualists who claimed to roust the bespeckled patriot from his eternal slumber and receive messages from him.

As related earlier, Leah allegedly conjured up the great inventor and introduced him to Charles Livermore. But that was only one of many, many times that name dropping Spiritualists brought forth Benjamin Franklin's spirit.

There were some things that even Sir Arthur Conan Doyle had trouble swallowing. He expressed doubts about the belief among Spiritualists that the rapping sounds "had been devised by the contrivance of a band of thinkers and inventors upon the spirit plane, foremost among whom was Benjamin Franklin, whose eager mind and electrical knowledge in earth life might well qualify him for such a venture."

Doyle wasn't certain that the spirit of Benjamin Franklin was leading a cadre of ghosts communicating with the living world, but he refused to dispute it outright. In fact, he related a story about the dead founding father in which two members of the Fox family were involved. Like many of the stories Doyle related, this one had gone through many tellings and retellings before he learned of it.

As has already been related, the notoriety of the Fox girls hatched a horde of mediums that, like so many locusts in a wheat field, laid waste to the gullible. One of the many, many minor mediums was a woman from Rochester called Mrs. Draper. According to Doyle, on February 12, 1850, Mrs. Draper went into a trance and had an interview with Benjamin Franklin.

The person questioning her asked the entranced Draper if she saw anything. She responded that she saw a stranger whom she had never seen before. She continued that the stranger wasn't "prepossessing in appearance," but that he was "very elevated in his position, in a reflecting attitude, and is busily employed."

Draper said the stranger was preparing work for the world, and he would communicate by rapping sounds.

When asked if she could identify the stranger, she answered, "Benjamin," then after a considerable pause, she said, "Franklin."

The interrogator then asked if the spirit could prove it was really Benjamin Franklin. There was a pause for about two minutes and then the woman appeared to go into spasms.

The questioner asked if the woman was coming out of her trance. She replied that she wasn't. Then she explained that she wanted a signal from the spirit that it was Franklin, and she asked for it to shock her. She then received a strong electric jolt, but she wasn't injured.

Draper continued that Franklin would communicate with her again on February 15, but he had conditions. The spirit demanded that Maggie and Katie Fox, Reverend A. H. Jervis, and a few other Spiritualists be present.

On February 15, the Spiritualists were assembled and Mrs. Draper tried to contact Franklin and receive a message from him. However, the séance was only a partial success.

Draper wasn't dissuaded. She was determined to make another attempt at communicating with Franklin. On February 20, she brought together another collection of Spiritualists, including: Margaret Fox and her daughters Leah, Maggie, and Katie; Reverend A. H. Jervis and his wife; Draper's husband; a Mr. Willetts; and a Mr. Jones.

Some of the participants were late, but when they finally arrived, Mrs. Draper supposedly contacted Franklin's spirit almost immediately. The spirit ordered them, "Hurry; first magnetize Mrs. Draper," and it was done.

Magnetizing a medium involved causing a trance in a passing by her, touching her, and focusing one's concentration on her. Magnetizing was an oft used practice that Spiritualists believed helped them connect to the spirit world.

The medium, now in a deep trance, told her audience that Franklin chastised them. She continued that he told her the tardiness of some put them behind time. She said Franklin would forgive them this one time, but that they must do better in the future.

The participants were split into two groups. Jervis, Margaret, and Leah were directed to a room, then the two doors between them and the parlor where Mrs. Draper sat were closed and locked. The remaining people at the séance stayed in the parlor.

Very loud sounds, like Morse Code, were heard in each room by everyone. The sounds frightened Katie Fox, and she called out, "What does all this mean?"

Although she was supposedly in a trance, Mrs. Draper answered Katie, "He is trying the batteries." The truth was that even though Franklin coined the phrase "battery," true batteries weren't developed until a decade after Franklin died.

Shortly thereafter, a signal was given for Franklin to spell out a message, and the spirit didn't disappoint. The message produced was "Now I am ready, my friends. There will be great changes in the nineteenth century. Things that now look dark and mysterious to you will be laid plain before your sight. Mysteries are going to be revealed. The world will be enlightened. I sign my name, Benjamin Franklin. Do not go into the other room."

A few minutes later, Reverend Jervis came into the parlor. He said the sounds directed him to come in and compare notes. The message he received was exactly the same as that which those in the parlor received.

Of course, there was no possibility for any group members to deny that Franklin's spirit was not present. That would have thrown Spiritualism into disrepute, and they couldn't have that.

The only real question that was never answered was why would Leah allow her sisters to take part in aiding one of their Spiritualist competitors? Perhaps, she felt that the publicity would help draw more people to their performances, but there's no way to know for sure.

There were many other accounts of Benjamin Franklin communicating with Spiritualists. Judge John W. Edmonds wrote that once blank sheets of paper were on a table and the invisible spirit of Benjamin Franklin made itself present in the company of two other spirits. Then suddenly, "a pencil got up of its own accord and wrote five lines of ancient Hebrew." Evidently, Edmonds couldn't read Hebrew; he didn't relate what the note said.

While Franklin was the celebrity most often mentioned by mediums as being present, there were many others. Hundreds of messages were received which were supposed to come from famous people, such as George Washington, Thomas Paine, Socrates, Plato, Sir Isaac Newton, John Milton, Galileo, Aristotle, Shakespeare, Lord Byron, Thomas Jefferson, the Apostles, Persian King Artaxerxes, Buddha, Zoroaster, Confucius, Moses, King David, King Saul, Solomon, Joan of Arc, Queen Elizabeth, Sir Walter Raleigh, the Czar of Russia, Abraham Lincoln, Louisa May Alcott, Susan B. Anthony, Enrico Caruso, Theodore Roosevelt, and others.

The name dropping began immediately after the Fox girls became famous. On February 26, 1850, the editor of the *Rochester Daily Magnet* related a matter "well worthy of investigation."

The editor stated that there handwriting samples from many famous people from years gone by. Some of those doing the writing were said to be the spirits of Benjamin Franklin; John Hancock; Phillip Livingston; Roger Sherman; John Adams; Stephen Hopkins; George Washington; Samuel Adams; John Quincy Adams; Charles Carroll,; Martha Washington; Robert Morris; Lewis Morris; Robert Fulton; William Henry Harrison; John Turnbull; Dolly Madison; James K. Polk; Andrew Jackson; John Penn; William Penn; James Madison; Thomas Jefierson; James Monroe; Henry Knox; Nathaniel Green; Alexander Hamilton; Richard Henry Lee; James Edgar; Edgar Allen Poe; John Paul Jones; William Dickinson; James Hull: and many, many others.

If the ridiculous assertions that the spirts of great men and women mentioned were really writing to mediums in such volume as reported, there wouldn't have been any paper left in Rochester. Nor would the spirits have had any time to do anything else during their eternal residence in the ether world.

13. Abe Lincoln and Other True Believers

From the beginning, there were thousands willing to accept the Fox sisters as genuine Spiritualists. Thanks to them, or rather, their promotion by their sister Leah, Spiritualism quickly became the fastest growing religion in the world. By 1851, there were more than one million Spiritualists in the United States alone.

The leading proponents of the movement weren't uneducated, unintelligent rabble, as their opponents often implied. They were, for the most part, well-educated, well-to-do members of the upper crust of society, especially in England.

Spiritualist leaders were certain in their beliefs. They were so sure that their faith was well-grounded that they were willing to expend substantial amounts of time, money, and energy in defense of their cult. However, they weren't willing to brook any criticism. They believed that those who disagreed with them for any reason were committing blasphemy.

Sir Arthur Conan Doyle's activities have already been documented in this volume, but there were many, many other famous people who embraced the cult. This brief chapter mentions several of those famous Spiritualists who fell for the trickery of the Fox sisters and other frauds.

Eliah W. Capron and Henry D. Barron of Auburn, New York, were true believers. From almost the beginning, they wrote extensively in support of the Fox sisters.

The two men claimed to be victims of those with which they disagreed. They claimed that the Roman Catholic Church was the chief persecutor. But they proclaimed proudly that in their defense of Spiritualism, they had survived the "opposition of Priestcraft and Ignorance unawed and unharmed." They said those hurling the charges at them were "Infidels, Impostors and Money-graspers."

More inclined to quote Shakespeare than religious texts, Capron and Barron were devout Spiritualists, nonetheless. They also promised their readers that they would provide "proof as positive as possible, as the class of facts related are of that nature which we do not and cannot expect men to believe without the most positive testimony."

It has already been related that William Crookes "investigated" Katie and declared her to be a true medium. However, even most Spiritualists described Crookes as gullible. He refused to change his opinion of any medium, even when the medium was caught using trickery.

The previously mentioned Judge John W. Edmonds was an avid Spiritualist, but he claimed to conduct an unbiased investigation of mediums. He wrote about an investigation that took place on August 1, 1853, but he didn't write the full story until March 13, 1859. He wrote superficially about levitation, table tilting, and "other violent movements of tables and chairs, ringing of bells, and so on."

Edmonds also wrote about a personal encounter he had with the Spiritual world. He stated that after testing mediums for weeks, he was in bed alone one night when he heard rapping on the floor. The strange sound moved from one part of the room to another with great speed. Next, he felt the rapping on his left thigh. Edmonds had experienced nerve twitching before, and he first thought that was what he was feeling.

He said he tried to prove the rapping was natural. "I sat up in bed, threw off all clothing from the limb, leaving it entirely bare. I held my lighted lamp in one hand near my leg, and sat and looked at it. I tried various experiments. I laid my left hand flat on the spot — the raps would be then on my hand, and cease on my leg. I laid my hand edgewise on the limb, and the force, whatever it was, would pass across my hand and reach the leg, making itself as perceptible on each finger as on the leg. I held my hand two or three inches from my thigh, and found they instantly stopped, and resumed their work as soon as I withdrew my hand."

Then, according to Edmonds, the rapping "ran riot" all over his body. He described "a storm of touchings from my left big toe, all the way up my leg to the upper part of my thigh ... This storm ran up and down my leg several times in a perfectly straight line."

The Edmonds story was deficient in several areas. He was all alone and there were no witnesses. Additionally, there were plenty of causes for what he felt, not the least of which was that he may have been having a dream.

The greatest problem in Edmonds' 1859 account was that it contradicted the account he jotted down in his diary in 1853. The diary entry said nothing about any rapping on the floor.

The description of his thigh being touched differed too. Edmonds wrote: "Tonight, after I had gone to bed, and while I lay reading ... I felt a touching on my left thigh."

He wrote nothing in his diary about the raps moving to his hand when he laid it flat against his thigh. In fact, he wrote that when he touched his thigh with his hand, the rapping stopped.

He did not mention in his diary anything about the rapping stopping after he held his hand two or three inches from his thigh.

The diary was also different in that he didn't state that the rapping "ran riot" over his body.

Some famous women such as Harriet Martineau and Elizabeth Barrett Browning were said to be enthralled by the Fox girls, and they were soon counted among the army of the Spiritualist cultists.

Shortly after March 31, 1848, interpreting rapping sounds became the preferred method of discerning spirit communication with the living. American abolitionist and Spiritualist Isaac Post was an important defender of the Fox sisters. He created a method of spelling out words based on the rapping sounds, and it became a standard text for mediums.

Some of the more obvious fake Spiritualists embarrassed even the most devout true believers. The Spiritualist cult was plagued by what Doyle called "swollen-headed ranters who imagined themselves to be in touch with every high entity from the Apostles downwards, some even claiming the direct afflatus of the Holy Ghost and emitting messages which were only saved from being blasphemous by their crudity and absurdity."

One community of these fanatics, who called themselves the Apostolic Circle of Mountain Cove, particularly distinguished themselves by their extreme claims and furnished mounds of material for the enemies of Spiritualism.

Doyle said that the great body of Spiritualists turned away in disapproval from such individuals and groups as the Apostolic Circle, but were unable to prevent the damage to the movement they caused. Of course, Doyle would never admit that the great body of those that didn't embrace Spiritualism found no difference between the fanatics and other fakers, such as the Fox girls.

Following the first séances of the Fox sisters in 1848, mediums sprang up all over America and Europe like so many mushrooms grown in the dark amid moist piles of manure. Only a few of these parasites gained any notoriety.

One of the most prominent and conspicuous Spiritualist con men was Scotsman Daniel Dunglas Home (pronounced Hume). He fleeced the gullible with such skill that he made Leah and her sisters appear to be amateurs in comparison. Not only was he a master bunko artist, but he was as slippery as a greased pig in avoiding the clutches of the police.

Home was handsome, suave, a good dresser, and convincing. His hook was that he didn't charge for his services, but he would "reluctantly" accept "unsolicited" donations.

Home was a teenager living in Connecticut when the Fox sisters began their hoax, and he decided to emulate them. He embarked his career as a professional medium in 1850, and before he was finished, he had traveled across the Unites States and Europe. He even performed for the Emperor and Empress of France, and the Czar of Russia.

Home was such a successful thief that in January 1867, he was able to trick an English widow named Lyon out of £30,000. About a month later, Mrs. Lyon asked for her money back, but Home ignored her.

Even though Home was utterly corrupt, the forever gullible William Crookes, as he had with the Fox girls, declared the charlatan genuine. Others that vouched for Home were the aforementioned Judge Edmonds, author William Cullen Bryant, and American Episcopal prelate Bishop Thomas M. Clark of Rhode Island

Famed British poet Robert Browning exposed Home as the "vulgar fraud" he was. Browning, who was concerned about his wife's belief in Spiritualism, went to Home and asked him to communicate with the poet's son who had died in infancy, and Home agreed. When a face appeared, Browing grabbed the materialized head and found it to be Home's bare foot. By the way, Browning never lost an infant child.

Despite being thoroughly exposed, Home continued his lucrative career for many years.

Efforts to prove Spiritualism scientifically were few, but one major figure in the scientific community did lend his name to experiments on the subject. Dr. Robert Hare was a medical doctor, sometime Professor of Chemistry at the University of Pennsylvania, and an Associate Fellow of the American Academy of Arts and Sciences.

In 1853, Hare conducted experiments with several mediums. In 1854, Hare converted to Spiritualism. He authored several books on the subject and became famous in the Spiritualist community. In 1855, he published a book titled *Experimental Investigation of the Spirit Manifestations*. His work was condemned by scientists but Spiritualists were enthusiastic in their support of it.

Traditional scientists opined as to why a scientist with such credentials as Hare would be convinced by what he saw at séances. They didn't believe he was incompetent, a dupe, or even gullible. They believed that Hare had strayed from his area of expertise, and that it was a fatal mistake.

Hare believed his expertise in observation in a laboratory setting gave him the ability to judge the validity of a séance. The problem was that mediums were exceptionally good at cheating. Scientists are trained to base their theories on what they see, and a man with Hare's background was simply unable to discern the tricks created by sleight of hand and distractions.

A trained magician with years of experience proved to be much better at debunking fake mediums than a gullible scientist was. Harry Houdini later proved that.

This chapter concludes with the stories of President Abraham Lincoln witnessing the powers of spirits during séances. Sometimes, the séances were conducted in the White House,

Mary Todd Lincoln was a devout Spiritualist. After her eleven-year-old son Willie died on February 20, 1862, Mary and the President attended several séances, at the White House and elsewhere, conducted by an alleged medium named Margaret Ann Laurie, as well as other "mystics." Laurie was one of the well-known "Georgetown witches," a circle of Spiritualist mediums in Washington.

The President and Mrs. Lincoln attended a spiritualistic séance in the Red Room of the White House in December 1862. A Miss Colburn was the medium on that occasion and President Lincoln said to her, "My child, you possess a very singular gift; but that it is of God I have no doubt. I thank you for coming here tonight."

Then on February 5, 1863, Lincoln and the First Lady attended a séance at the home of Margaret Ann Laurie and her husband Cranston, in Georgetown. This somber affair was broken up by a comical episode.

The mediums were Margaret Laurie and her daughter Belle Miller. During the séance, Laurie directed that Miller place her hand on the piano, and when she did, "the piano rose and fell a number of times."

A "quaint smile" crossed the President's face and he said, "I think we can hold down this instrument." The gangly fifty-three-year-old Republican climbed atop the piano. As the President sat upon the instrument with his legs dangling over the side, former Congressman Daniel E. Somes, railroad tycoon Simon Peter Kase, and a Major serving in the Army of the Potomac, joined the President on the piano.

Perhaps no greatest collection of Americans ever sat on a levitating musical instrument together at once. However, they failed to accomplish their purpose. Despite the weight added to the piano, it continued to wobble and move about until the President and his aides grew tired of their ride and bailed off it.

After the séance ended, Somes said to Lincoln, "When I relate to my acquaintances, Mr. President, what I have seen tonight, they will say, 'You were psychologized and you did not really see it.'"

The President reflected for an instant, then he replied quietly, "You should bring such a person here and when the piano seems to rise have him slip his foot under the leg and be convinced by the weight of evidence resting upon his understanding."

In April 1863, the President, the First Lady, and several of their friends, including Cabinet members Secretary of the Treasury Gideon Welles, and Secretary of War Edwin Stanton, attended a seance in the Red Room at the White House. The room contained a new grand piano made by the Schomacker Company of Philadelphia. It had been delivered to the White House around June 1861, and the Lincoln children used it in their music lessons.

The new piano didn't dance around the room, but at this séance, a note was left by the supposed spirit of America's first Secretary of War, Henry Knox.

Evidently, Knox wanted to advise Lincoln on military matters. If so, he didn't help much. The Civil War ground on for another two years.

There was another séance in the Red Room in the winter of 1863-1864, which the mystic Colburn hosted. Apparently, it was uneventful.

The President was present at another séance which Mrs. Colburn hosted at the White House later in 1864. Nothing of note happened on that occasion either.

Some sources contend that Lincoln didn't believe in Spiritualism. They are of the opinion that he was merely curious. Yet, it is hard to believe that Lincoln attended or even allowed séances at the White House if he believed they were hoaxes. It is known that Lincoln was superstitious, and that once he had a madstone applied to his son Robert Todd Lincoln to keep the lad from acquiring hydrophobia.

14. Harry Houdini vs. Spiritualism

DURING the first quarter of the twentieth century, Harry Houdini was the greatest escape artist and magician in the world. He was also the world's greatest opponent of the fakery practiced by Spiritualists. He wasn't a contemporary of the Fox girls, but he spent a great deal of time investigating their methods. He proved conclusively that they could have tricked the true believers, even without outside help.

Houdini wrote, "Like most perplexing things when made clear, it is astonishing how easily it is done. The rappings are simply the result of a perfect control of the muscles of the leg below the knee, which govern the tendons of the foot and allow action of the toe and ankle bones that is not commonly known.

"With control of the muscles of the foot, the toes may be brought down to the floor without any movement that is perceptible to the eye. The whole foot, in fact, can be made to give rappings by the use only of the muscles below the knee. This, then, is the simple explanation of the whole method of the knocks and raps."

Houdini testified before Congress from February 26 through February 29, 1926, and he provided incontrovertible evidence of several Spiritualist hoaxes.

The great magician and his assistant Rose Mackenberg exposed many fraudulent mediums. Some of the fakers they exposed were:

Joaquin Maria Argamasilla, also known as the "Spaniard with X-Ray Vision." Argamasilla claimed he could see through metal. Houdini publicly exposed him as a fraud by demonstrating that Argamasilla was merely peeking into the box to see what was inside.

The medium Jane B. Coates used the honorific "Dr.," although she had no credentials. She was a well-known Washington, D.C., Spiritualist. She headed the Spiritualist Church of America, also known as the Spiritual Science Church of Christ and the White Cross Church of Christ. She began practicing in the

District of Columbia in 1921, and she soon built up an impressive clientele, including many government officials. Houdini exposed Coates during his congressional testimony.

"Margery" (Mina Crandon) was a member of the upper crust. Her husband was a prominent Boston surgeon. She was a contender for the $2,500 prize offered by *Scientific American* magazine for anyone who could demonstrate genuine psychic abilities under test conditions. She may have won had Houdini, who was a member of the magazine's investigative committee, not exposed her. He proved the spirit ringing a bell was actually Margery ringing the bell with her foot. He also proved she used her dentist's thumbprint to produce "spirit" manifestations in wax. Houdini even published a pamphlet called *Houdini Exposes the tricks used by the Boston Medium 'Margery'*, which detailed Margery's cheating.

Madam Grace Marcia was another of those Houdini exposed for her deception. Marcia claimed after the fact that she foresaw both Warren G. Harding's election and his death. The dispute between the psychic and the magician led to death threats against Houdini.

Eusapia Paladino was an Italian who occasionally refused to accept money payments for their seances – but she never turned down "voluntary" contributions. According to Houdini, he proved Palladino cheated in several cities, including New York. However, the Spiritualists continued to believe that she was genuine, and they supported her until her death in 1918.

Nino Pecoraro was exceptionally good at deception. In three séances before the *Scientific American* committee in which Houdini wasn't present, Pecoraro was convincing. But Houdini attended the fourth séance and bound Pecoraro with a custom restraint. Pecoraro was unable to produce any "psychic phenomena," confirming Houdini's suspicions of fraud. In 1931, Pecoraro confessed he had tricked his audiences.

Hatfield Pettibone was a "physic psychic" from Boston, He traveled the world as a missionary for the Spiritualist cult. Pettibone continued his proselytizing even after being debunked by Houdini.

The most noted example of Houdini debunking a fraud ruptured his friendship with Sir Arthur Conan Doyle.

Even though Doyle and Houdini disagreed about Spiritualism, they had remained friends for some time. Doyle's second wife, Jane, was as devout a

Spiritualist as her husband. She claimed to be adept at automatic writing. Sir Arthur convinced Houdini to allow Jane to try to contact Houdini's mother.

On a specified day, Jane sat across a table from Houdini. She then took a pen and began to scribble on a blank sheet of paper. When she filled one sheet, Jane continued to the next. When she finally put down her pen, Jane had a fifteen-page letter in excellent English that she said Houdini's mother had written to him.

The world's greatest illusionist had several problems with the so-called letter. First, Jane had made a cross on the upper portion of the first page. Houdini knew his Jewish mother would never make a Christian cross on any letter she wrote.

Another problem was that his mother was proficient in Yiddish and German, but she could hardly speak English, and was unable to write it at all. Had the message been written in Yiddish or German, it may have had a chance of convincing Houdini.

Then, there was the fact that the letter referred to Houdini as "Harry." The magician's mother never referred to him by his stage name; she always called him by his given name, Erik.

Doyle tried to convince Houdini that the message was real. The novelist said the cross wasn't a Chistian symbol, it merely represented a religious presence. As far as the message being written in English, Doyle gave two possible explanations:

First, although he didn't mention it beforehand, Doyle told Houdini that mediums often translated messages dictated to them from the spirit into their own languages. This would also account for the message using the name Harry instead of Erik.

Second, Doyle stated that the spirit of Houdini's mother may have learned English on the other side. He didn't explain why a spirit would need to be multilingual.

The absurd explanations Doyle offered didn't convince the great magic man. Besides that, Houdini learned that his wife, Bess, had engaged in a conversation with Jean Doyle shortly before the séance. Jean had pumped Bess for information about Houdini's mother. Sure enough, the information Bess provided wound up in the message from the other world. It's a shame that Bess couldn't teach Jean to write in Yiddish.

Houdini all but called Jean a fraud, and Sir Arthur was deeply offended. After that, Doyle and Houdini became polite enemies. While they never engaged in personal arguments, they battled it out in various newspaper editorials.

Even though Doyle continued to criticize Houdini after the magician's death, he remained convinced that his former friend was no mere prestidigitator. Doyle always held that Houdini possessed the supernatural powers of a true medium. Doyle believed that Houdini knew it too, but that the magician had just been too proud to admit it.

Houdini's vitriolic relationship with Sir Arthur Conan Doyle and others within the Spiritualist movement led to fears that fanatics might try to silence him.

There were stories that Madam Grace Marcia had predicted that the great Houdini would die on Halloween night in 1926. When the supposed prophecy came true, there was speculation that somehow Spiritualists had murdered their nemesis. There was a brief investigation into Houdini's death, but no evidence was ever produced to indicate that the great magician's death was due to anything other than natural causes.

15. Others who Exposed Spiritualists

HOUDINI was not the only person of note that refused to accept the parlor tricks performed by the Fox girls and the horde of mediums that followed them. Many peered through their antics, and from the beginning, pronounced the Spiritualist cult an outright swindle.

The opponents of the Spiritualist mediums didn't consider them leaders of a competing religious movement that deserved tolerance. In fact, their opponents didn't have any respect for the Spiritualist mediums or their cult at all. They considered the self-proclaimed mystics to be nothing more than leeches – charlatans who preyed upon the gullible. They could see no middle ground between themselves and the Spiritualist hyenas, and they said so.

As early as 1850, critics concluded that the Fox girls were making the rapping sounds themselves. One of those critics was noted physician E. P. Longworthy. Longworthy investigated the Fox sisters and noted how the knocking and rapping sounds always came from under their feet or when their dresses were in contact with the table. He concluded that Maggie and Katie had produced the noises purposely.

As was related in Chapter 6, towards the end of 1850, three professors from the University of Buffalo developed the theory that the Fox girls were simple frauds. The educators understood that the alleged otherworldly rapping could be caused by the girls cracking their knee joints. They placed the girls' legs and feet so no cracking could occur and no ghostly rapping happened. However, the failure of the Fox girls didn't diminish their popularity.

In articles he wrote for the *New York Times*, John W. Hurn came to a similar conclusion of fraud as the Buffalo doctors had.

Several religious leaders offered explanations as to how the Fox girls performed their tricks. Naturally, adherents to the Spiritualist cult felt the traditional religious leaders were backwards reactionaries.

Reverend John M. Austin concluded that the Fox girls could make the rapping sounds by cracking their toe joints. Austin was later proven correct.

Reverend D. Potts demonstrated to an audience that the raps could be made by cracking joints.

As related in Chapter 7, the Reverend C. Chauncey Burr was a severe critic of the Fox girls. In 1851, Burr wrote in the *New York Tribune* that by cracking their toe joints, the Fox girls could make sounds so loud they could be heard in a large hall.

It wasn't just men of the cloth who doubted Spiritualism generally, and the Fox girls specifically. Men of science were also skeptical.

One of the chief skeptics of Spiritualism was Charles Grafton Page. Page was an electrical experimenter, inventor, physician, patent examiner, and patent advocate. Page's background made him adept at detecting and exposing fraudulent claims. In 1853, he authored a book called *Psychomancy*. Page pointed out that the rapping sounds produced at their performances came from underneath the girls' long dresses.

The Seybert Commission was a group of faculty members at the University of Pennsylvania who in 1884–1887 investigated a number of respected Spiritualist mediums, including Maggie. The Commission uncovered fraud, or suspected fraud, in every case that it examined.

With Maggie, the Seybert Commission determined that the phenomena associated with her were produced by fraudulent means. Their report noted that the raps were heard close to Maggie and séance attendee Professor Furness had felt pulsations in her foot.

French lawyer and doctor, Dr. Joseph Maxwell, studied mediums and mystics of all kinds for many years. He found all the mediums he investigated, including the Fox girls, to be frauds. During his investigations, he identified six different fraudulent ways of producing spirit rapping.

Dr. Maxwell proved by conducting a large number of experiments that loud raps could be made by knee and toe joints, which was the way the Fox girls produced them.

Maxwell stated strongly that séances held in total darkness were a waste of time. Cheating was too easy in the darkness. Mediums could use their feet or hands, or a concealed stick to make noises in the darkness. Some mediums even had electrical devices hid under their clothes that they could pull out and use under the cover of darkness.

Dr. Maxwell challenged Spiritualists who didn't believe him. He said that since the spirits could rap on floors, walls, doors, or chairs, that there was no need to use a séance table, and it should be removed. He said the only reason for a séance table was to cover the cheating.

Maxwell said that he could be convinced if the medium was "plainly isolated, and bound in limb and joint" and the mysterious raps still occurred. Maxwell never heard a rap during such a test.

16. The Role of John and Margaret Fox

THIS chapter briefly examines the role John and Margaret Fox may have played in the fraud upon which modern Spiritualism was built upon. It is necessary because in the past 175 years, no one has seriously considered the fact that they may have played a vital part in the confidence game.

The elder Foxes were considered decent, honest people, but they were not believed to be sophisticated. As such, it was thought they could be fooled easily – especially Mrs. Fox. But were they fooled, or were they doing the fooling?

Harry Houdini unfairly called Margaret Fox, whom he never met, "simple minded." Others called her a "nervous, superstitious woman." But was she what she was believed to be? Or was she feigning simple-mindedness to gain an advantage?

John Fox and his wife Margaret were members of the Methodist Episcopal church, and there was nothing on the surface to imply that they were in any way involved with the occult before March 1848. But a deep dive reveals something different.

As was related earlier in this volume, the Fox family never attended any church regularly except for Maggie, and no one in the family ever became a practicing Christian. Even then, Maggie did not become devout until in adulthood when she rejected the Methodists and became a Roman Catholic.

Eliab W. Capron commented that "the church" attacked Margaret Fox and forced her to "give up" her former faith. The truth is that the Spiritualist faith and Christianity are incompatible. Therefore, Margaret Fox could not be a Spiritualist and be a Methodist simultaneously. She had never been much of a Methodist, and considering that Spiritualism provided her livelihood, it was an easy choice for her to join the Spiritualist cult.

Previous chapters made various mentions of Margaret Fox and her relationship with her girls. Most of those that made statements about her were positive, and none thought she could have had any involvement in the flimflam. However, there are some things that indicate she may not have been as innocent as previously supposed. In fact, she may have been a major player from the beginning.

Leah said that when she saw her mother in May 1848, Margaret was completely broken down by the events. Leah said of her mother, "She never smiled; but her sighs and tears were heart-rending." That was utterly untrue. Margaret spent a considerable amount of time on stage with her daughters, and she was all smiles most of the time. It was even reported that Margaret Fox's hair turned white within a week after the incident on March 31, 1848.

The truth is contrary to what Leah said. If Margaret was so upset, why was she a willing participant in many of the shows the girls held? Why didn't she make any strong effort to protect them from the mass of gawkers?

Margaret wrote, "I am not a believer in haunted houses or supernatural appearances. I am very sorry there has been so much excitement about it. It has been a great deal of trouble to us. It was our misfortune to live here at this time; but I am willing and anxious that the truth should be known, and that a true statement should be made. I cannot account for these noises; all that I know is, that they have been heard repeatedly, as I have stated. I have heard this rapping again this morning, April 4th. My children also heard it."

Margaret said she didn't want publicity. If that was true, why did she bring in neighbors to witness the event? Maggie said that Margaret caused the hoax to spread unintentionally, by calling in the neighbors to see the girls communicate with the spirit world. But was it unintentional?

Former Indiana congressman Robert Dale Owen was a true believer, but he advised Margaret Fox not to publicize the gifts her girls possessed. Margaret didn't take his advice. In fact, she did the opposite of what Owen advised.

Considering the fact that she was the leading questioner on the first night, it seems likely that she was in on the prank early on and took advantage of it.

There is ample evidence that Margaret did have a big part in the hoax. She admitted in her statement of April 1848 that she was the first to question the spirit. She started by asking the ages of her children, then went from there. The later questioners repeated most of the ones she had already posed to the spirit. Therefore, Margaret must have been feeding questions to the later questioners.

Even if Margaret Fox wasn't a part of the fakery at first, she embraced it rather quickly after the money came flowing in. She took an active role in the performances put on by the girls.

There were persistent charges that John Fox was the architect of the fraud. It was pointed out that the spirit raising at Hydesville was so skillful, continuing for several weeks, that it caused a commotion and made the Fox girls famous. But how was it possible?

Henry Montgomery relayed the discovery that John Fox had made the "miracles" possible. According to Montgomery, Fox had created "an ingenious arrangement of springs, wires, etc., was enabled to make a great variety of supernatural sounds, and to get up many wonderful sights, such as the locomotion of chairs, tables, books and other household fixtures."

Whether or not John Fox had created a system of sound-making devices is still disputed. However, it would explain how the rapping could continue after the girls left to spend the night with a neighbor.

An undeniable fact is that after the girls became famous, neither John nor Margaret ever worked again. They were cared for by Spiritualists and by the income their daughters generated. As related earlier in this volume, Horace Greeley opened his New York City residence to them. John, it seems, lived there full-time, and Margaret lived there when she wasn't on the road.

The story of the haunting on March 31, 1848, seems so contrived as to cause doubts about everyone involved. Was it staged to bring notoriety to the girls? Was it a test run designed to see if the girls could fool locals before taking the show on the road? If so, it worked marvelously, and it could never have succeeded without the active participation of John and Margaret Fox.

Perhaps the strongest indication that John and Margaret Fox were deeply involved in the hoax was in how they treated Maggie and Katie. Much has been written about the characters of John and Margaret Fox, but they certainly failed in their duties as parents. It appears that they, as was Leah, were more interested in the girls' money generating power than they were of protecting their children from the vultures circling them. In fact, it appears that the parents were vultures, too.

Even though she went on the road with them and took part in their performances, Margaret Fox took little motherly interest in caring for Maggie or Katie after they gained notoriety.

She seemed not to care that even as teenagers, they drank heavily. In fact, she would have had to provide alcoholic beverages to Katie, because she was practically the only adult to have access to the child. One might suppose that Margaret felt Katie was easier to control if she was drunk much of the time.

But Margaret did her best to keep her young girls working and earning a steady income. Their performances provided for her livelihood.

Treated like a freak show act, with no parental supervision or protection, and with no friends their own ages, it is little wonder that Maggie and Katie, like celebrity children sometimes do, fell into self-destructive behavior.

Lonely, exhausted, and without parental support, Maggie and Katie were virtually forced to take up drinking when they were still teenagers. That they soon suffered from alcoholism seems a logical outcome for the poor Fox girls. The true believers, such as Sir Arthur Conan Doyle, blamed the constant drunkenness of the girls on "some family disposition towards alcoholism," and on the "captious, grumbling crowd of investigators" hounding them.

The Spiritualists never considered that the pressures from parental neglect, overwork, and overpowering guilt may have pushed the girls toward the alcohol abuse.

John and Margaret Fox could have stopped the grumbling crowd of investigators any time they wanted to stop it. They could have put an end to the performances, taken her girls home, and let their children live normal lives. Sadly, John and Margaret had other priorities.

17. The Spiritualist Cult Survived

ONE might assume that after Spiritualism's founding prophets admitted their hoax, the cult would collapse. It didn't. Religions are resilient; they persevere. Some people still worship Odin, and others still worship Zeus. It should be no surprise that Spiritualism survived – at least to a degree.

In the four decades between the first toe click by the Fox girls and their confessions, hundreds of apostles and millions of adherents around the world had taken up spiritualism. The mere fact that their beliefs were based on flimflam didn't dissuade the true believers.

Naturally, there were those that didn't believe the confessions of Maggie and Katie, and there were others who simply tried to rationalize them away.

One reason the Spiritualist cult has achieved permanency is because it is attractive to a certain kind of people. Spiritualism doesn't associate itself with morality in any way. The cult is founded on the belief that human spirits are immortal, and that there is no permanent punishment for their actions while they were in the living world. As Doyle put it, it makes no difference if when alive a person was "a drug-taker, a dipsomaniac, or a pervert ... The individual's character has nothing to do with the matter."

The belief is that some spirits are placed in the lowest "circle" in the realm of the dead, and those spirits have to learn better behaviors to advance to higher circles and move nearer to the deity. But since they aren't suffering in purgatory, there is no hurry for them to be promoted. After all, they have an eternity.

The Fox sisters – even Leah – have never been disowned by Spiritualist true believers. On the contrary, the Fox sisters are still considered prominent figures in parapsychology, and are widely cited in Spiritualist literature.

Most of the Spiritualist authors recount the stories of March 31, 1848, but ignore the many times that unbiased observers laid bare the fakery practiced by the three Fox girls.

Another reason that Spiritualism has survived is that few of the critical accounts of séances have been preserved. Even today, as one would expect, the

Spiritualists tend to tout the positive and ignore the negative. If one looks at Spiritualist websites, for instance, he will find much about the Fox girls, all of it positive.

While today the Spiritualist cult has only between ten and twenty percent of the membership it had at its peak a century ago, it appears that it will stay with us for the foreseeable future.

Before leaving this topic, it must be pointed out that some Spiritualists never adopted it as a religion. They wanted to use the spirits for profit. As one person wrote, "impostors, have taken advantage of the public demand for Spiritualistic excitement, to fill their purses with easily earned guineas." However, the same author stated that "others who have no pecuniary motive for imposture are tempted ... solely by a desire for notoriety."

Some people were only interested in the movement to the degree that spirits could be employed as fortune tellers. These Spiritualists inquired about such things as to the winners in upcoming elections, what financial investments to make, what horses to wager on, or whether to pursue a certain love interest.

Exactly how the belief that spirits could read the future came about is uncertain.

Conclusion

THERE is no active anti-Spiritualist movement today, and voices from the past describing the theater of the mediums as "trickery of the most trivial and vulgar kind" are not commonly repeated.

There shouldn't be any such movement. People should be allowed to follow their beliefs without fear of persecution from mobs toting pitchforks and brandishing whips. That being said, those that know the truth shouldn't swallow it. If a belief cannot continue in a truthful world, it will fail on its own, without suffering the slings and arrows of any persecutor.

The story of Maggie and Katie is certainly a cautionary tale – a terribly sad story.

Neither Katie nor Maggie lived into old age. Katie died in 1892 at the of 55, and Maggie, who was 59, died the next year.

Leah, who had caused her sisters so much agony, proved the cliché that the wicked don't die young. She lived into her 78th year before passing away in 1890.

Even though both Maggie and Katie married, they lived lonely lives. They earned the equivalent of millions of dollars, but they both – especially Maggie – suffered from the pangs of poverty. Despite being among the most famous people of their time, they died in obscurity.

What started as an innocent prank led to a personal disaster for the girls, and to millions of trusting people who were led down a treacherous road paved with deceit.

Selected Sources.

"Bones in 'Old Spook House.'" The Boston Journal, November 23, 1904.

Capron, Eliab W. *Modern Spiritualism*. New York: Partridge and Brittan, 1855.

Capron, Eliab W., and Henry D. Barron. *Explanation and History of the Mysterious Communion with Spirits*. Auburn, New York: Capron and Barron, 1850.

Coleman, Benjamin. *The Rise and Progress of Spiritualism in England*. London: Beveridge & Fraser, 1871.

Doyle, Arthur Conan. *Our American Adventure*. New York: George H. Doran Company, 1923.

Doyle, Arthur Conan. *Our Second American Adventure*. Boston: Little, Brown, and Company, 1924.

Doyle, Arthur Conan. *The Case for Spirit Writing*. New York: George H. Doran Company, 1923.

Doyle, Arthur Conan. *The Edge of the Unknown*, reprint. New York: Barnes & Noble Books, 1992.

Doyle, Arthur Conan. *The History of Spiritualism, Volume 1*. London: Cassell and Company, 1926.

Doyle, Arthur Conan. *The History of Spiritualism, Volume 2*. London: Cassell and Company, 1926.

Doyle, Arthur Conan. *The New Revelation*. London: Hodder and Stoughton, 1918.

Doyle, Arthur Conan. *The Vital Message*. New York: George H. Doran Company, 1919.

Doyle, Arthur Conan. *The Wandering of a Spiritualist*. London: Hodder and Stoughton, 1921.

Doyle, Arthur Conan, Joseph McCabe. *Verbatim Report of A Public Debate on the Truth of Spiritualism*. London: Watts and Company, 1919.

"Exposing Spiritualism." *The Daily American*, October 22, 1888.

Gammon, CL. *Mad Stones: Their Use in Middle Tennessee, and Elsewhere*. Lafayette, Tennessee, Deep Read Press, 2025.

Gammon, CL. *The Queen and King of Hell in Salem*. Lafayette, Tennessee, Deep Read Press, 2020.

Hare, Robert. *Experimental Investigation of the Spirit Manifestations*. New York: Partridge & Brittan, 1855.

"Hatfield Pettibone Dead." *Dayton Herald*, May 11, 1904.

Houdini, Harry. *A Magician Among the Spirits*. New York: Harper & Brothers, 1924.

Houdini, Harry. *Houdini Exposes the tricks used by the Boston Medium 'Margery.'* New York: Adams Press Publishers, 1924.

Kahler, Abbott. "The Fox Sisters and the Rap on Spiritualism." *Smithsonian Magazine*, October 30, 2012.

KJV Holy Bible. "1 Samuel 28:7-25." Nashville: Thomas Nelson, 2017 (1607).

New York Herald, April 17, 1851.

New York World, October 21, 1888.

Page, Charles Grafton. *Psychomancy: Spirit-Rappings and Table-Tippings Exposed*. New York: D. Appleton and Company, 1853.

Podmore Frank. *Modern Spiritualism, Volume 1*. London: Methuen & Company, 1902.

Tyson, Philip John; Dai Jones; and Jonthan Block. *Psychology in Social Context*. Malden, Massachusetts: John Wiley & Son, 2011.

Underhill, A. Leah. *The Missing Link in Modern Spiritualism*. New York: Thomas R. Knox & Company, 1885.

About the Author

CL Gammon has had a life-long fascination with the written word. This fascination has led to his authoring more than 70 books.

Gammon, studied Political Science at Tennessee Technological University and History and Government at Hillsdale College

Over the years, Gammon has received several prestigious honors and awards. He has twice received the Certificate of Appreciation for Service to the State of Tennessee (2018 and 2025), the Partisan Prohibition Historical Society Citation of Merit (the only two-time recipient), and nomination for the 2023 Gilder Lehrman Lincoln Prize.

Several universities, including the State University of New York, the University of Akron, and East Mississippi Community College, have utilized his books as course material.

Articles written by Gammon have appeared in more than a dozen national and regional publications. He has also written feature articles for his hometown newspaper, *The Macon County Times*.

CL Gammon lives in Lafayette, Tennessee.

www.ingramcontent.com/pod-product-compliance
Lightning Source LLC
Chambersburg PA
CBHW070541080426
42453CB00029B/794